The Wit and Wisdom of Charles E. Bradford

The Wit and Wisdom of Charles E. Bradford

Compiled by William and Noelene Johnsson

Review and Herald® Publishing Association
Washington, DC 20039-0555
Hagerstown, MD 21740

Copyright © 1990 by Review and Herald® Publishing Association

The author assumes full responsibility for the accuracy of all facts and quotations as cited in this book.

This book was
Edited by Penny Estes Wheeler
Designed by Bill Kirstein
Cover photo by Joel Springer
Type set: Optima

PRINTED IN U.S.A.

95 94 93 92 91 90   10 9 8 7 6 5 4 3 2 1

Texts credited to Anchor are from *The Anchor Bible*, copyright © 1971, 1974 by Doubleday & Company, Inc.

Texts credited to NIV are from the *Holy Bible, New International Version*. Copyright © 1973, 1978, International Bible Society. Used by permission of Zondervan Bible Publishers.

Bible texts credited to TEV are from the *Good News Bible*—Old Testament: Copyright © American Bible Society 1976; New Testament: Copyright © American Bible Society 1966, 1971, 1976.

Library of Congress Cataloging-in-Publication Data
Bradford, Charles E.
    The wisdom and wit of Charles E. Bradford / compiled by William and Noelene Johnsson.
        p.   cm.
    1. Bradford, Charles E. 2. Seventh-day Adventists—United States—Clergy—Biography. 3. Adventists—United States—Clergy—Biography. 4. Seventh-day Adventists—Doctrines. 5. Adventists—Doctrines. I. Johnsson, William G., 1934-   . II. Johnsson, Noelene, 1938-   . III. Title.
BX6193.B66A3   1990
286.7'092—dc20   90-8238
[B]   CIP

ISBN 0-8280-0585-0

CONTENTS

Preface	7
Roots	9
On Being Black	26
My Ministry	41
The Church	54
The North American Division	61
Preaching	63
The Ministry	88
"Get This Message Going" (Speech to the 1989 Annual Council)	95
Anecdotes	101
The Sabbath in Africa	111
Ethel	114
"You Will Be Missed" (Sermon at Charles L. Brooks' Funeral)	117
Sermons	128

IN APPRECIATION

He is one unique person!

My dear friend Brad is best characterized as a dynamic preacher, natural orator, impromptu speaker. He has the ability to weld a disparate crowd of people into an action-oriented group, he displays amazing recall of stories and appropriate illustrations to diffuse tension and fit every special situation, and above all, he is an inspiring and trusted leader. All this, and much more, is what Brad means to me. Twenty years of close association with my esteemed colleague has etched the profile of his life on my mind and memory screen in a way that can never be erased.

—Neal C. Wilson

PREFACE

At the farewell reception for his secretary, Sheila Potter, Elder Charles E. Bradford was delayed and missed the beginning. Explaining his absence, he said, "When I was in Chicago they introduced a song, 'God Is Still on His Throne.' There was a little boy in the congregation who thought that the song said, 'God is still on the phone.' Well, the brethren are still on the phone."

Anyone who has heard "Brad" speak knows that he possesses stunning oratorical abilities. He is able to quote anecdotes appropriate to the situation at a moment's notice, and his humor—always gentle, always in good taste—defuses tense debates, pricks bubbles of pomposity and shallow argument.

And he is a preacher par excellence. Brad is at home in the pulpit as are few other Adventist ministers.

This is a book about Brad—the man and his wisdom. Throughout these pages, Brad is the speaker. We are merely compilers of his ideas and wit.

Although this book does not attempt to trace Brad's biography, the outline of his life emerges, but not in order—his roots, the formative influences, his ministry. We pieced the manuscript together from many hours of conversation with Brad himself, and also from the recollections of various friends and colleagues who supplied us with anecdotes. In particular, we are indebted to Calvin Rock, Brad's nephew; Owen Troy, communication director of the North American Division; and to Gary Patterson, Brad's assistant.

Others donated their services in typing the manuscript:

Corinne Russ, Jeanne Jarnes, Carol Smith, Cheryl Show, Lois Bellis, and Barbara Huset.

Royalties from this book are being given wholly to a project chosen by Brad himself—research into the history of the Sabbath in Africa. Brad has a hunch, based on Ellen White's brief comments in *The Great Controversy*. But find out from Brad himself within the following pages.

In his preaching, in his ability to turn a phrase, in his penetrating wisdom and spontaneous anecdote, there is none like Brad in the Seventh-day Adventist church today. By this book we seek to honor this man who has done so much to glorify the Master and to build up His people in our times.

Roots

My Mother

My mother exerted the greatest influence on my life. Dad was a good man and I loved him, but my mother was more gentle and kind. In later years I found out that my father wasn't all that tough, but he would never let us see him cry or anything like that. He was the disciplinarian.

Mother could discipline us also, but she was very, very kind. Everybody thought she was a saint. I was with her a great deal because Dad was always away giving Bible studies and preaching. He read his Bible aloud every morning after worship—he read it through 70 times. But he was away so much, because he had three churches.

So I spent a lot of time with my mother. She would tell me stories, but she was always sure to get the Sabbath school lesson in. We just had to get in our Sabbath school lesson and the memory verse. Sometimes when she would come home at night and I was sleeping, she would wake me up and say, "We've got to get the memory verse." The next morning I would get up and recite the memory verse, but I couldn't remember when I'd learned it.

My mother was a nurse. She trained in the New

England Sanitarium, going there after Oakwood. Some of her family became Adventists under Edison White on the Mississippi, and so they sent her to Oakwood. She was just a girl and Oakwood was only an elementary school then—maybe a little more, a training school. That's not to put it down, because in the South after the war and during reconstruction and a long period after that, older people were trying to catch up. They had wanted to read all their lives, so you would see moms and dads and uncles and aunts in class with kids. It was probably one of the greatest responses to an educational opportunity in history—a whole people involved in learning.

Well, Mother went to Oakwood, and when she got everything they had there somehow she got up to New England Sanitarium. Her cousins went to Battle Creek, but she got to New England somehow.

During that time, in the early 1900s, Kellogg was still in the church. When he came to Melrose, everybody had to clean up the place because he was a cleanliness nut, fastidious.

Ellen White visited the San when my mother was there and they asked her, "Would you like to be Sister White's chamber girl?"

She said, "Oh yes." So she waited on Ellen White. I have no great revelations that Sister White gave her, no prophecies or predictions. She said once that Sister White mentioned she was interested in the Oakwood school and wanted to see it prosper, but she didn't talk a great deal. Ellen White was not a great talker at that stage of her life—she wasn't all that young. My mother went to Boston with her when she preached there.

Some of us feel that Ellen White's speaking influenced my mother. Mom was what they called, in those days, a dramatic reader. It was a big thing then. They would have soirees—evening programs—and they would say, "Mrs. Bradford will recite," and she would recite some Biblical passage or poem. I remember her public readings.

I suppose she influenced my own public speaking—although not consciously. I admired her speaking because she was capable of projecting her voice in round tones in a very pleasant way and everybody liked to hear her. In fact when Pop was away and she had the prayer meeting, some would say that he could stay away a little longer if he wanted to.

Eva

My sisters taught me a lot since I was the youngest. They were in high school. I tease them now that I suffered under them.

Eva, Calvin Rock's mother, was the one I always wanted to stay with me. But I would call her Ida, because I couldn't say Eva. That would make her angry, and she would say, "You always call on me."

When I learned the Lord's Prayer, I didn't understand what I was praying, and I used to say, "Deliver us from 'Eva.'"

Growing Up in the South

I didn't live in the south until I went to Knoxville, Tennessee. My dad was pastor there for a couple of years, and I must have been about 10 years old at the time.

I was looked on as a stranger in the Black community. You see, coming from the north I talked like a northern kid. I didn't understand southern mores and customs. I had to undergo a little taunting every now and then—not bad, but people would say, "Here he comes. You know, he's from up north." Many Blacks from the north had a superior attitude, looking down on Blacks from the south as being in quasi-slavery.

The funny part of it is that the southern Black had really more in some ways than the northern Black because he owned a little property. The northern Black hardly had any property, was renting a room or apartment at best. And the southern Black had a culture and a society that was headed by the preacher, the teacher, the undertaker, the doctor—those people in the community who were really looked up to.

The preacher was the top dog. In some places the teacher was very high, especially if he was a high school principal. If perchance you had a college in the community, the president was really somebody. There were more Black teachers in the south because the schools were segregated. In Philadelphia where I lived as a boy for a while, the schools were supposed to be integrated, but there were very few Black teachers. They didn't have a cadre of them, or any support system for a fellowship of teachers. But in the south they had many, and some good ones.

At that time the church in Knoxville couldn't have been more than 50 or 60 members, and it was the largest Black church in the district. I don't know about Chattanooga, because we never visited any others outside our district. In those days a hundred-mile journey was a long trip. You had to get up early in the morning and pack a big lunch. It was really a safari, and almost always you had a flat tire.

Formative Years

My formative years were spent in New Rochelle, New York. Every year, the Greater New York Conference used to have a rally day, a convocation for the whole conference. Everybody came together and we would meet in the Brooklyn Academy of Music. It was an adventure to go from New Rochelle on the train—first the Interurban down to New York—and then on the subway all the way to the Brooklyn Academy of Music. They would always have someone like Elder Spicer or Elder McElhany come to preach. It was a memorable day; we would take a lunch and so on.

In the New Rochelle church we had a few Caucasians because there was no White church in the county. I remember one Captain Roberts, a sea captain, who was a member. There were several White members in that church, and nobody treated them any differently, nor did they treat us differently. They were fine old people, and we never thought of them as being different, and, of course, being a child I did not think about it. The schools were integrated—I did not go to any segregated schools when I was a boy. I went to the public schools, nothing else, no home study for kids, so my parents prayed and put me in public school. My father was interested in education, so I went to the public school and was well treated there.

They were the kind of White people who were not threatened by Blacks—gracious people, genteel society people. I went to school with those kinds of kids in my early days, and the school principal was a fine gentleman who would ask if we were being treated right.

My mother was vice-president of the PTA. She was a dynamic speaker in her own right, so she made things better for our people in the Lincoln school there in New Rochelle.

We would go almost annually to the Pennsylvania camp meeting. Greater New York had no camp meeting, and Dad was well known in Pennsylvania. My parents would rent a tent and Dad would put Mom and me on the train and we would go to Wescosville, Pennsylvania. In those days there were two conferences in Pennsylvania— East and West. Wescosville was kind of a little village. We had our camp meeting at a place called Eden's Grove, and we used to go out on the "Toonerville Trolley." There were just a few Black people there in those days.

Of course, there were no Regional conferences yet. Was I made to feel welcome at camp meeting? At that time

I was not sophisticated enough to be able to reflect on it, I just acted. As a child I didn't know any strangers. I was in and out of people's tents and cabins, and I didn't feel that there was racial prejudice or that type of thing at camp meeting.

One day when Mother and I were going from New York to Allentown on the train, the conductor came through and said, "Bethlehem! All out for Bethlehem!"

I shouted, "Oh, Mother, this is where Jesus was born!"

Everyone in the whole coach smiled. Everybody thought that was so cute.

Father

My father was a very strong man, an evangelist and a pastor. He was involved in education, though—he taught. He and Mom told me they started a boarding school in Arkansas way before I was born. It had just a few students.

Southwestern Union looked them over, but they didn't give them very much to go on. My dad and mom went to the union session and made a great appeal for one cow—if they could get just one cow the work could go on. There my mother contracted malaria and almost died; that was a tough experience for them. In later years I met people who went to school under Mom and Dad there in Arkansas.

In his preaching my father was very fundamental, Biblical. He was a great expository preacher; he took advantage of the headlines for prophetic interpretation. I remember him as a strong disciplinarian. He was a patriarch, no question about it.

His family was from Alabama originally, but they migrated to Kansas City, Kansas, because in those days there was money in cattle, and packing houses were big. You can trace the migration of Black people in several ways. This was one of the first waves—the 1890s, I suppose. Cotton had worn the land out and they couldn't make a living. Things were oppressive, so people would just pick up and go—migrate, walk all the way to Kansas. Kansas was considered free territory since they had never had slavery, while Missouri was not.

My dad's father became an Adventist from reading one of our books. They had been Presbyterians. Now, the Presbyterians had a big program of education for Black people in the south. They were very active, founding a string of high schools and two or three colleges for Blacks.

Those of our family who remained in Alabama were educated well by the Presbyterians. One of them, my cousin, now retired, became librarian of Atlanta University, and another, a Dr. C. Eric Lincoln, became and still is one of the top scholars in the nation. He wrote a definitive study on the Black Muslims. But my granddad went to Kansas and became an Adventist and, of course, he heard of Oakwood College and sent my dad there.

Many good White people felt a debt toward Black people—many from the Boston area, where abolition was big. They went south. That is a great untold story. Scores of young White people from the best families went south and lived their lives out in those communities teaching Black people. They were, of course, ostracized from the rest of society.

This was after the Civil War. That's why Ellen White urged our people, "You get in there." She was telling us we could clean up if we would just go there and do something. And she said the Black people's living should not depend on cotton. They should be taught trades, business, all the rest. But we were rather slow.

Rich Friends

In New Rochelle, New York, we had no church school—we could not have one. That was a rich city, a bedroom suburb for New York City. My brother used to caddy for Lou Gehrig and Babe Ruth at the Westchester

Country Club. Not for them together, because they hated each other.

I went to school with rich kids. I didn't know them well, but they had the most wonderful toys, like big fire engines you could get on and ride. They weren't rough-and-tumble streetwise kids, and I wanted to protect them. If anybody would beat up on the little kids, I was always chunky and heavy and bigger than my age, and I would lean on the boys who tried to hurt them. The kids were so grateful for me that they would give me some toys.

Dad's Asthma

My dad had terrible asthma. He went through some awful times—all the doctors—nobody could help him.

Then somebody gave him an asthma cigarette. If he smoked this he would be OK—the aromatic spirits would help, you know.

I burst into the room one day—he would go upstairs, I guess, and try to get away from everybody—and there is my dad smoking. He did not actually have it in his mouth; it was on the saucer. He was trying to inhale it this way. He was afraid, I guess, to put it in his mouth.

I wanted to die. It was a very dark day in my life. I thought my father was smoking, and there was no use for me to live. It was the end.

Then Dad saw that I saw, and he explained everything to me. Even so it took some time to wear off before I could look at him again.

Mother Cunningham

When I first went to Oakwood as a high school student in the early 1940s, it was just becoming a senior college. Mother Cunningham was there then. What a wonderful saint she was!

She became an Adventist in Natchez, Mississippi, or

ROOTS

one of those towns, and went to Oakwood, and she never left it until she died. She became matron, married a gentleman there, and had one son who was an educator.

Mother Cunningham touched everyone's life who came through Oakwood. Dedicated to her work, she was serious, a most awesome person. We boys, mischievous as we were, would say, "Boy, if anyone's going to heaven, it's Sister Cunningham, she's the one."

She could look through you and almost read your heart, or so we thought. She loved young people, though. She had that stern front but every now and then she would ask you to dinner on Sabbath. And she would say, "You can do better than that, even the girls eat more than that."

Mother Cunningham was a hard worker and had a garden. Once when I was playing ball—and "they" could always quote Ellen White, you know; she said that play isn't necessary—Mother Cunningham stopped me and before I knew it had me hoeing that garden. After she worked me nearly to death, she took me in and gave me a big dinner.

It was an event whenever you went to dinner at her house. The school was small in those days, and by the time of commencement almost everybody had had at least one meal in her home.

Mother Cunningham could give a good talk. Once when she was talking about the potential of young people and how much is bound up in them, she looked over at me, and said, "Charles, you are wonderful, but you just don't know it."

The kids razzed me for weeks. They would come up to me and say, "Charles, you are wonderful, but you just don't know it."

I was embarrassed, but I knew she meant well. She was trying to tell me that if I would just wake up and shape up, I could do something. That was Mother Cunningham, a great influence in my life.

She ran the laundry, was matron of the girls, ran the dining room for a while, was even boys' dean one time. She was a spiritual mother for the whole campus.

At times we even heard her chide the president. He had a very hearty laugh and she would say, "Now, Frank, you are the president and you shouldn't laugh like that in front of the students." She could do it and get away with it. She was another Ellen White in a way—that kind of mother—and she would give a little rebuke now and then. But what a great saint and role model!

J. L. Moran

When I was a student at Oakwood College, the president was J. L. Moran. He had been principal at the Harlem Academy in New York, the school started by Humphrey. But he came to Oakwood College as the first Black president. At first they refused to call him the president, principal was enough. But it wasn't long before he earned the title president.

Moran was a doer, a shaker and a mover. He was also a thrifty man. The kids called him "king" for King Kong, because he walked bent over a bit and his arms were a bit long. He didn't like it, but they did it out of his earshot. He was strong as a bull. None of the fellows dared challenge him physically.

O. B. Edwards

O. B. Edwards also was at Oakwood when I studied there. He was a scholar, the quintessential college professor. A historian, he read with emphasis, his sentences all correct. He was a stickler for discipline. Term papers had to be punctuated correctly, with no cross-outs or anything. We had to write everything by hand in those days. Edwards would give us back our papers and we had to correct them, even the smallest mistake. He was great on essay tests. He was one of the few Blacks who went on and got a doctorate, receiving it from the University of Nebraska.

What a great man he was! And a musician and a poet. He even wrote the school song.

George E. Peters

George E. Peters was another person who influenced me greatly. He wasn't a teacher at Oakwood, but a pastor in the field. He was a preacher of preachers—Uncle George they called him.

Peters came from Antigua in the Caribbean. He was sent to New York to save the situation after the Humphreys split off. Man, could he make an appeal! He was an intense man, always saw himself in hand to hand combat with the enemy.

Peters was elected secretary of the colored department, but they didn't want to give him an office in the General Conference. So Elder McElhany, who was the General Conference president said, "Brother Peters, you just bring your desk into my office," and soon they found an office for him.

Eva B. Dykes

Eva B. Dykes was one of those people who helped to make Oakwood. She had a strong influence on me and on many others.

She received her Ph.D. degree from Radcliffe the same day as Teddy Roosevelt's daughter. She was probably the first Black woman to receive a Ph.D. in the United States: another woman received hers the same day, but she was farther west, in another time zone, so they call Dr. Dykes the first.

Her uncle was an elder of the church and a tremendous educator and leader in the community. He was a man of great dignity, and he pushed her. She went on to teach at

Howard University in its heyday. At that time Oakwood was trying to get accredited. They needed people with doctorates on the staff. They had been after Eva B. Dykes for years, and finally she decided to cast in her lot with Oakwood College. That was an event.

Eva B. Dykes was baptized as a young person. Her uncle brought her into the church. She kept very faithful, unashamed of her faith, witnessing on the Howard campus. I know a man in her class who became an Adventist. He was Professor N. E. Ashby, who also became a teacher at Oakwood College.

Dr. Dykes taught English at Oakwood. She insisted on the proper usage of the English language, no sloppiness. She would point out a preacher in a minute: "Young man, if you are going to be a minister standing and speaking to the people, you must do better than that, now." She wasn't browbeating people, she was just showing the way and inspiring them, molding them.

Dr. Dykes was a musician too. She practiced a couple of hours every day.

She never married, although she had a lot of suitors. She, like the apostle Paul, was too dedicated to her profession and to young people. I suppose marriage would have been in her situation, as Paul says, a hindrance to her.

Eva B. Dykes had a lot of young people who looked upon her as mother and friend, and we all remember her fondly.

F. L. Peterson

Frank L. Peterson was president of Oakwood after Moran. He retired as a vice-president of the General Conference.

Peterson was baptized as a promising young man in an evangelistic effort in Pensacola, Florida. He had been marked for greatness in the Methodist church. He was a musician and a tremendous speaker.

Peterson went to Oakwood, then on to Pacific Union College, where he graduated. He was one of the few Black ministers at that time to have a college degree. Later he was elected secretary of the North American Regional Department. That department, by the way, had been named and renamed. First it was the Negro Department, then the Colored Department, then the Regional Department.

As president of Oakwood, F. L. Peterson was a father figure, leader, educator, and pastor rolled into one. He had the respect of all. He built that school from his own personality.

Peterson was a great singer—he sang his way through Pacific Union College. He wrote a book called *The Hope of the Race*—a subscription book that kids sold in the summers to make money.

F. L. Peterson had witticisms and a sharp tongue at times. In conversation if you got in a verbal joust with him, you might just as well throw up your hands, because he was so quick and alert he would cut you to ribbons—in a nice way, you know. I enjoyed that.

But when he spoke at chapel, it was an event. They used to talk about a sermon he gave one Sabbath—"The Symphony of Life." I wasn't there—I'd already graduated—but I heard all about it. Peterson was a great influence on all of us.

Calvin E. Moseley

Another character that impressed me tremendously was Calvin E. Moseley. We called him "The Rabbi." He was the Bible teacher. He molded the preaching and ministry of almost every Black minister in North America for a generation. C. E. Moseley still lives. After retiring from the General Conference as a field secretary he returned to Oakwood and teaches an occasional class.

Moseley's sermons were deeply spiritual, solemn occasions. He knew how to put the fear of God into his audience. We thought he was hard on us ministerial students. Tie pins were "pride blossoms." But he knew how to teach homiletics. He used Evans' book How to Prepare Sermons and Gospel Addresses. Any Oakwood ministerial student from that era can tell you how to use the What, Why, How, and What Then in preparing a topical sermon.

He was never known to waffle on any issue. He would tell you in a minute if he didn't think you could make it. And in spite of the fact that he very rarely gave high recommendations to anyone, he loved his preacher boys, followed their careers with great interest, helped them all that he could in their ministry. But again I must admit, even before James Dobson, he epitomized tough love.

The Depression

My dad went on retirement benefits early, when I was still a kid. Those were the depression years. Father spent years working under pressure, sometimes misunderstood. He was a man ahead of his time. Wherever he could, he would start a church school. It was a sadness in his life, a sorrow, that he could not get one going in New Rochelle. The county wouldn't let him have it: in such a high-class county, they weren't about to let any little parochial school move in.

Times were hard. The conference would give a brother a box of books and say, "Brother Bradford, that is your salary for this month." It was like that.

Ellen White spoke about kingly power, and she knew what she was talking about. Kingly power was exercised in those days, but my dad was not a person to say, "Yes sir," and bow. He had a bit of Mordecai in him. So he had a little difficulty with the brethren.

Then he took ill with heart trouble. After he would preach on Sabbath, he would come home and Mother would have to prop him up on pillows. Being a nurse, she just about kept him alive.

ROOTS

Finally he had to retire, and we spent some time wandering about. We went to Oakwood College and stayed with Sister Cunningham, and I was in school. The little sustentation my dad received didn't take care of us, so we were glad to be at Oakwood because my brother and sister were there—Terrence and Vera. Then we went to Tennessee and stayed there for a while.

We wound up back in Philadelphia, Pennsylvania. My father had practically founded the Black work there, but that was in 1918 and 1919. He said he wanted to do something, and they gave him a little company to take care of.

We went to Ebenezer church, however. That is another one of those Biblical names. Ellen White in one place says that the young people should get a name to work under. A name rallies people: "I belong to Ebenezer," and so on.

Elder Thomas M. Rowe was the pastor of Ebenezer then. We had some characters in the ministry in those days—strong men, terrific preachers. Rowe was a tall, gaunt looking man, but he preached with refinement. I enjoyed him.

My dad began bringing in some money by renting rooms. There were homes there, row houses just like today in Philly, with absentee landlords. You could rent a house for $25 or $30 a month, cut it up, and put a kitchen on the second floor and so forth, and rent it out. The landlords didn't care about sub-letting. The landlord just wanted a little money. You could tear the house one way or the other, change walls, and collect the rent.

The house we lived in was a big, big house. We rented rooms there. We lived on one floor and rented out two floors.

So my dad had to do all these things to make a living. We also sold eggs, oranges, ripe fruit people would bring us, and *Message* magazines.

One redemptive feature was that my mother was a

nurse. Dr. Kimbrough was a friend and she would say, "Sister Bradford, come over and help me. Help the patients give their history and work with them."

My mother and Dr. Kimbrough wrote the first practical nurses' course in the city of Philadelphia. They used to bring in Battle Creek and New England medical people. They would have big classes at the church. Practical nursing was a big thing then. The community came in and they graduated 30 or 40 people at a time. This was before the days of nurses aides, and she and Dr. Kimbrough foresaw all that. I have seen the manual they prepared. They had little white dresses and caps and things they gave the people. Non-Adventist people remembered them for a long time.

All this was in the late 30s and early 40s.

"I'm Black."

It was my mother who gave me a sense of self-worth. As I've already told you, we lived for some time in New Rochelle, New York, and I attended the Lincoln School both in kindergarten and the first four grades. Being a minority kid, I was sometimes the butt of taunts and jokes by a few of the students. "Here comes the ole Black boy," I'd hear. "Blackie! Blackie!" I don't know that they intended to be especially cruel, but you know how children are. And you also know how a sensitive little boy can feel.

My mother saw, without my even telling her, that this was affecting me. One day she drew it out of me. I blurted out, "They're calling me 'Black' and making fun of me because I'm Black."

She smiled. "Of course you are, and so is your dad. And he's the finest man that I know. He has never raised his hand to strike me. He never uses bad words. You can be proud to be like him."

The next day when the litany began, I held my head up high and gave my mother's little speech. "Of course I am,"

I said proudly. "I'm Black, just like my dad. And he's one of the best men in the world."

And that was the end of that.

Mother's Death

My mother died from appendicitis. Her appendix was evidently in the wrong place in her body and the doctors were baffled. She knew very well from the pain that the appendix was the problem. To make matters worse, the doctors had no wonder drugs—the penicillin all went to the army.

Poor mother lived a month or five weeks in terrible pain. They took fluid off her by the gallon. The doctor said, "She is strong. If this had not happened, she would have lived to be 100." What a tragedy!

I was in school and I came home to see her. At that time they had given Dad a little church in Harrisburg, Pennsylvania. I had just decided to be a preacher. That made mother happy—you know how mothers are.

Now, you have to take what follows with a grain of salt, but my sister Vera tells me that it definitely, positively happened. She and all the girls were there. Mom and the girls had great fellowship together.

So the sad family sent for me and I got on the train and came home from Oakwood. My dad said, "Well, son, you preach on Sabbath." And I preached. My sisters say they told Mother that I was going to preach. I think that she heard that sermon, even though she was in the hospital. She was very, very ill, with her last illness. She never came home from that hospital. But she thought she heard me preaching. She said to people who came to see her, "Don't say anything." She was listening as if she were in the audience that day.

My sister Vera tells me that over and over again. Apart from that experience—which is sort of mystical—my mother never heard me preach.

On Being Black

Ephesus

People have often wondered why Black Adventist churches name themselves according to Biblical places, not after persons. You won't find any St. Paul's, St. Peter's, or St. John's, but you will find Black SDA churches calling themselves Shiloh or Berea or Ebenezer, and so on. But the favorite name is Ephesus because it is first in the list of the seven churches.

In the early days of our work the conference office or the treasurer's office or whoever made up a list of churches would always name the Black church—or as they called it the "colored" church—the "number two" church. So "number two" became a code for Black.

But there came a time when Black people felt that was inappropriate. They were unhappy with it, so they protested in the best way they could, and that was by naming themselves from Biblical cities, et cetera. Ephesus was the one they chose more than any other because it was believed it meant "first." So, you will find an Ephesus church in New York; one in Jacksonville, Florida; another in Columbus, Ohio; and others scattered throughout the country. There was even one in Washington, D.C., in the early days.

Humphrey Movement

I was born in Washington, D.C., but afterwards we moved to the New York area, ultimately settling in New Rochelle, just north of New York City. New Rochelle in West Chester County is a bedroom suburb of New York City, and at that time West Chester County was the richest county in the United States and in the world, with many New York financial leaders living there. The New Rochelle church was the only Adventist church in the county. My father became its pastor—it was a church of 75 to 80 members, medium size for those days.

The big church at that time was in Harlem, New York, the Ephesus church. That church grew out of the Humphrey movement.

Humphrey was a Jamaican who came to the United States shortly after the turn of the century. He had been a Baptist minister, but became a Seventh-day Adventist and started work among the Black people in Brooklyn. He pastored the Ephesus church for 20 years, and it became an institution in itself. In fact, from it came an academy—Harlem Academy.

Elder Humphrey left the church—defected—and began his own movement, which he called the United Sabbatarians, or something like that. He and my father were great friends and he tried to persuade my dad to join his movement, but of course my dad didn't.

Humphrey split off from the Adventist church about 1929 or 1930, just before we came to New Rochelle. The brethren sent Elder George E. Peters to New York. He came from Chicago, where he had done a great work, building the Shiloh church. They asked him to go to New York and hold the church together, because Humphrey took with him about 700 people or more, including some of the most talented and educated.

Humphrey's movement was strong at that time, but Elder Peters was a powerful evangelist and he rebuilt the membership. They began renting the Dutch Reform church in Harlem, at 123rd and Lennox. The name "Harlem," you know, comes from Holland and Harlem was originally a silk stocking neighborhood in New York where Dutch people lived. The Dutch Reform church was empty because of the changing neighborhoods, and our congregation under Elder Peters rented this property. It was a big stone and marble building with a tall steeple, one of the landmarks of the city. Peters preached and evangelized the city, and the church filled up. He left it with about 1,000 members, which was huge for those days.

Remnants of Humphrey's movement still exist today. These men were strong leaders, and Humphrey was the daddy of them all. He wanted to build Utopia. He felt that he needed a health retreat for Black people and more educational facilities—he had already founded the Harlem Academy. He felt Blacks needed opportunities in business to become involved in community work more effectively, so he bought, without conference approval, a property in New Jersey. He called it Utopia and they were going to have a big center. They even composed a hymn, "Utopia." That made a great stir.

Humphrey established work in Newark, New Jersey, and other cities, including St. Louis, Missouri—they had a little church there and I met them when I went to St. Louis in the 1950s. In New York City itself there are still several churches that have come out of the Humphrey movement.

Only to Memphis

Mississippi is my mother's state. She was born in Vicksburg. Mississippi is known among Black people as being one of the most difficult places. Dyed-in-the-wool segregation. Just to mention the word conjures up all those pictures of cross burnings and the rest. So I feel qualified to tell you this one:

A certain Civil Rights worker was on his way to Mississippi to assist in the voter registration drive. This was dangerous in any part of the South, but especially in Mississippi. And so it is alleged that he prayed, "Dear Lord, I'm going down to Mississippi to get the people registered to vote. Will You go with me?" To which the Lord replied, "Only as far as Memphis." (Memphis is just on the other side of the river.)

Volume 9

In Volume 7 of the *Testimonies* Ellen White speaks about the Black man and the White man being equal—their names being together in the Book of Life, that you shouldn't be ashamed to shake his hand on the street, and all of that. She makes wonderfully idealistic statements about Christ recognizing no caste.

But it seems that when she comes to Volume 9 she temporizes: she becomes pragmatic, practical. She monitors herself in her expressions and says in effect, "We can't do as if there were no prejudice here. It's a vexed question and always will be. I don't think the spirit of slavery is over." She makes some statements in Australia that sound almost despairing as she is discussing matters with the brethren in counsel. She says she doesn't know what's going to become of the country, tells our people that they can't do what they could in Michigan when they go down to Alabama or Mississippi. She says to let the colored people have their own places of worship, and not to cut off the ears of the White people by fraternizing too freely with Blacks.

Seeing the church as proclamation and missionary, she wanted to get the message out to all classes of people. That ideal community of equality would have to wait. In order to keep the doors of opportunity open, it would be necessary for the Blacks to be provided with meeting places of their own.

She also said that for many reasons White men should be the leaders. So she trims her sails—Volume 9 is quite different from Volume 7.

I haven't made a great definitive study of this matter, but my assessment—my resonance—is that conditions at the time she wrote Volume 9 played a major part in her counsel. We hadn't been in the south before, and now her own son Edison was there. Our work had begun in New England and had spread west, but it took a long while before we went south. We had very few believers there, and Ellen White was wondering how to reach the people. She could see that an interracial church simply wouldn't be acceptable to the white society.

Ellen White, it seems to me, was wise. Intermarriage— was counseled against when the topic came up. Talk about inflaming people!

Now until the 1920s and 1930s, when Blacks began to think about their position in the church and to protest against segregation, some leaders used her Volume 9 statements as frozen texts that were for all time. Many Black people were very incensed, and some lost their way over this. In order to remain Adventists, they had to develop a hermeneutic for interpreting Ellen White. The other alternative was to accept their status and be Uncle Toms.

So they got into it. Some of them said, "This can't be. Ellen White has done so much and is so far ahead—far ahead of even Lincoln that we just can't accept this as being for all time. The matter of church attendance, of marriage, of social relationships, of leadership—this can't be a text for all time. This is simply ad hoc counsel to save the church, to preserve its witness, but not to be used as a rule to govern the community of faith from here on to the Eschaton."

ON BEING BLACK

I think that's one of the main reasons that Blacks have not had as much a problem with Ellen White and her use of sources, et cetera. They have developed a hermeneutic for her: they look on her as a fine mother, a good counselor, but they could not take every word she said as being eternal in its application and universal for all time. They had to make some adjustment in it, or they could not remain Adventists and be honest people.

Volume 9 was being used as a club, a control factor. "Here, Brother Jones is getting too uppity. Don't forget what Sister White said in Volume 9!" So Volume 9 became almost an epithet in the mouths of Black persons: "Volume 9!"

Of course Ellen White made some statements that are hard to understand—like the amalgamation of man and beast. Not many of these statements, just a few. But in the hands of unscrupulous people they can be used to preserve racial supremacy. Not often, but every now and then, for instance when a Black kid and a White kid want to marry, we hear: "Volume 9!"

The Humphrey movement set the tenor of church social relationships in the 20s and 30s. Then came the 40s and events in the larger community greatly influenced the agenda. Blacks petitioned through the courts to order the secretary of war to consider their applications for enlistment in the army air corps as flying cadets. Mass meetings were held in 24 states to protest against discrimination in the national defense effort.

The National Urban League presented a one-hour program over a nationwide radio network urging equal participation for Blacks in the national defense effort. Transit companies in New York and Philadelphia agreed to hire Blacks as drivers and mechanics after boycotts and strikes. Then finally, President Roosevelt issued executive order 8802 which forbade racial and religious discrimination in war industries, government training programs, and government industries. All in 1941.

Things began to pick up in 1942 and 1943. The pressure was on. If Blacks could die for their country in foreign lands they certainly should be accepted at home as workers in defense industries. I remember well when Son, Ship, and Drydock Company first hired Blacks in other than janitorial positions. This must have been about 1940. Change was the order of the day. Intelligent Black laymen found the situation untenable. Enlightened White members shared their feelings. The Volume 9 mentality had to give way to a more enlightened social consciousness in the Seventh-day Adventist Church."

The following has a point.

They tell about a Black man who was the sexton, the old word for janitor or custodian, in an exclusive White congregation. They didn't allow him to sit in the auditorium but he sat outside the door and listened to the sermons. By and by the old gentleman was impressed—as they say, convicted and converted, born again. So he went to the pastor and said, "I'd like to join the church. Your sermons have got to me and I've come through."

"Well," the kindly old pastor said, "there's a Black church across town. Why don't you go and ask the Lord about joining there?"

And as the story goes, the dear old Black man did. When he came back the pastor said, "What about it?"

"Well, I still want to join this church. This is where I found the Lord."

The pastor asked him to pray again and he did. But when he came back this time and the pastor asked, "What about it?" he said, "Well, the Lord told me not to feel too bad because he's been trying to get into this church a long time Himself and hasn't succeeded."

Anna Knight

Anna Knight was a Mississippi girl who was trained by

Kellogg—she was pre-Oakwood. She went to India with a group of missionaries, and when she came back she became the colored educational superintendent for the Southern Union.

Anna Knight lived on the train, carrying a trunk around with her. She always wore a blouse (we called it a middy blouse in those days) and a little string tie. She was a preacher and took the pulpit on Sabbath.

Anna Knight was a nurse and an educator. She examined all the kids, would critique their classroom and work with the teacher, then would get on the train and go to the next place.

That's the way our schools were held together in the Old South, the Southern Union. It's a tremendous story. Those schools had a big influence in the growth of the work. At that time 85 to 90 percent of the Black people were in the south and rural areas, in the country, in small towns. These schools did a good work in reaching the people.

The Old South

In the old South, many Blacks and Whites often had the same name. On the plantation there would be the Black side of the family and the White side.

My mother's people were all mulatto, and she was a mulatto. So was Anna Knight, L. H. and Frank Bland, and many others I could name. My father, however, was ebony skinned, very dark.

My mother was so fair that she was often taken for White. In fact, she and Dad would be traveling in the South sometimes and an old sheriff would say, "This Black man bothering you?"

She would answer, "Well, I would like for you to know that this Black man is my husband!"

Whites were like that in those days, always watching for any union of a Black man and a White woman, and vice versa. Well, not too much vice versa—they took advantage of Black women all the time.

Edson White

The work in the South was opened up by Edson White. He and his crew came down with the boat they called "The Morning Star." They docked in Vicksburg, then moved up to Yazoo City. In Yazoo City, according to some, they docked the boat at the home of my mother's sister, Aunt Lucy, on the river.

My mother told me that they had a lot of music and singing on the boat, and that they invited the people to come. They preached from the landing.

At that time (1895-1900) they set up schools all through the South because everybody wanted to learn. It was almost like the English language schools in some countries today. Later Oakwood supplied the teachers for these schools.

By the early 1900s Oakwood was a "normal" school—that is, a training college for elementary teachers. In the South in those days a high school education was a big thing and anyone with a diploma could teach, with a little additional "normal" training.

Elder Brother

In the old South the White man always had some good Black friends, but they were not his equal. Good friendships but no social equality. He was like Albert Schweitzer, who said about the Africans in Lambarene, "The African is my brother, but I am his elder brother."

There was a kind of benign paternalism. Under this system Whites developed fondness for certain Blacks. But this never changed the more widespread customs and mores.

They used to tell stories about the civil rights conflict.

The old White fellow told the Black fellow, "Listen, when things get real hot and heavy and we have to shoot somebody, let's don't shoot each other."

State Troopers

I sometimes have had state troopers and other policemen just out to stop me. I once was very tired and the officers thought I was drunk. They found out I wasn't, but just tired. They saw the Bible and said, "Preacher, please pray for me, won't you. Now just go on and be careful, you hear?"

They were nice to preachers most of the time, but they could be fickle. They might be fine one time and in the same circumstance the next day cut your head off. All the same it was helpful to always keep your Bible very visible.

Two Different Worlds

I do not remember much prejudice against me personally. But one is aware of the climate, the atmosphere. One is also protected by living in another world with its own support system.

People have their own social world, and their own religious world, and they do not interface with the larger world except when they must do business in the larger community. At the Atlanta Exposition in 1896 Booker T. Washington held up his hand. The light was streaming through it in the afternoon—he was copper colored—and he said, "In all things social we are just as separate as the fingers on the hand. But in all things of common good we are just as one." That encouraged the Supreme Court to decide for separate but equal in the famous Plessy vs. Ferguson case.

In the Black community there was a cultured society making order, a dynamism. Humanity makes its way, and there you also had a more homogeneous community in that everyone lived together. You didn't have large neighborhoods of poor, or middle-class, or rich, or whatever. Everyone was in the same neighborhood—a better house maybe, but not a better neighborhood. Maybe on the better side of the neighborhood you would find the preacher, the doctor, the school teacher, one or two bankers here and there, insurance magnates. They had nice homes and sometimes servants, and they were a great influence on others in the community, role models.

The church was the life of the community when I was young. The church put on cultural programs—soirees, they called them. They got that word from the French. They would put on dramatic readings, skits, plays.

In New York the Harlem No. 2 church put on a play called "The Great Image," based on Daniel 2 and the Hebrew boys. My mother played Nebuchadnezzar—they put a beard on her! People came from miles around to look at that play. Several in the audience joined the church as a result. One became a minister.

People had activities. They had a life. They had goals. They had objectives.

Brothers

According to the old story, the slave owner said to the little slave, "I gotta teach you now. I'm going to Christianize you. Come, I'll teach you the Lord's prayer. Repeat after me, 'Our Father.' "

The little slave said, "Your Father."

"I said, 'Our Father.' "

He said, "Your Father. If He is our Father, then you are my brother. I can't imagine our Father being happy with the way you are treating your brother."

Christianity does that—it makes us equal. You just as well get ready to either accept this brother or shoot him, because he one day is going to live in heaven with you.

ON BEING BLACK

Jim Crow

During the days of slavery there wasn't any such thing as segregation. The master and the slave traveled together and even slept in the same room. They didn't have a colored section on the train and no separate drinking fountains. The valet traveled with his boss and his boss wasn't going to have him sit in another section of the train or steamboat.

But after the Civil War there was a social vacuum and they had to invent Jim Crow [segregation] to fill it. Jim Crow became a code word for legal separation. They had to preach it, until it became our way of life. Isn't it something how you can take the human psyche and twist it and make people believe that something existed from the beginning?

All this came about because of Reconstruction. It was so radical: White men came down from the North and put the Black man in as mayor, and so on. It was too radical for the times, and there was a lot of revenge in it. Then presidential candidate Rutherford B. Hayes offered the South concessions if they would vote for him.

So in the 1890s there was a rush to write laws. They wrote all the laws they could to separate Blacks from Whites and preserve White supremacy. Even the old southern families at first said, "This is foolishness. This is not the way we ought to do it." But the supremacists convinced them, and they did it by saying, "Do you want these Blacks to rule over you? Do you want them to marry your daughter?"

So Jim Crow was established. The freed men could be kept in their place. Things could go on as they had in antebellum times.

Then in 1896 we have the Supreme Court ruling on Plessy vs Ferguson, and the doctrine of separate but equal becomes law. That was a watershed. It gave Jim Crow a name, like giving life to the image of the beast. The old southern Baptist preacher said Jim Crow was the illegitimate child of slavery, but now they gave him a name and legitimized him. They made him acceptable in polite society, and so it became rigid, the order of the day. "Our way of life." The Reconstruction was over.

This was the time when Ellen White had to tell our people to be careful in race relations and when she wrote the statements of Volume 9. This also was the time when her son Edson was going down to the South to start the work.

Those were difficult days. I think there was at least one Adventist who was martyred, and some were tarred and feathered. If you were to come down from Boston to a little southern community, the first thing you would hear is, "Here is that _____ Yankee!" They didn't like you. Second, they would say, "He's messing with the heads of my plantation workers. Wants to give them Saturday off from picking cotton. I give them Sunday to go to church. What do they want—two days off from work? He's going to ruin my business!"

It was just like Paul when he was put in jail in Phillipi—he took business from the merchants by preaching against idols. So everybody jumped on the Adventists: the Black preachers and the White preachers, the politicians, and the landowners. It was a tough time to be either a Black or White Adventist in the South then.

Regional Conferences

You will hear some people say that the Blacks begged the White brethren for regional conferences, but it wasn't like that at all. In fact, it was the leadership who offered the Blacks their own conferences. Black people had always wanted inclusion—to be a part.

By the 1940s the number of Black Adventists had increased, and we had more and more who were educated. The whole world was moving in the direction of equality.

There were several things that kicked it off. One was an

ON BEING BLACK

incident involving a very fair-skinned woman by the name of Lucy Byard. She had pneumonia and they admitted her to the Washington Sanitarium. She was an Adventist. But after they found out that she was colored they shipped her out of the hospital and she died in another hospital. People were mad, angry: "What is this! Is this our church?"

Segregation—that's the reason I wasn't born in the Washington Sanitarium. When I first visited the General Conference, the cafeteria at the Review and Herald also was segregated—I couldn't eat there.

The proposal for regional conferences came from the White leadership—from Branson, McElhany, and Nethery. The Black brethren said, "We'd better take what we can get." Branson had worked in the South and he knew the mind of both Black and White. That's why the Black brethren loved him so much. McElhany was a little austere, but he was a fair man. Nethery was a pragmatist. He said, "Brethren, the time has come." So they made it an eschatological event—the time, the *kairos,* has come. McElhany said, "Look at our Black brethren. They have large churches and they administer them. They could administer conferences as well."

W. W. Fordham was the first president of the Southwest Region Conference. When I went to New Orleans he was the secretary of the Colored Department of the Southwestern Union. All of us knew it was just a matter of time before the Black work would be organized. W. W. was a great natural leader. We all looked to him to rally the troops and point the way. Evangelism was his forte. He was an orator, as they say, of the first magnitude.

The new organization was begun in his living room in Dallas, Texas. You should understand that before conferences were organized the Southern Union and Southwestern Union plan was to have a Colored Committee in each conference. The leading Black minister would be the secretary.

THE WIT AND WISDOM OF BRADFORD

Some conferences were most meticulous in their records of how the Black work was progressing. They would often say, "The colored work is in the hole." It is alleged that just before Southwest Region Mission was organized, W. W. and W. S. went to the conferences and demanded to see the books. In one instance there was a bit of consternation when the record showed $20,000 balance in the Colored Fund. This was an astronomical sum in those days and helped to get the fledgling organization on its feet.

Those were turbulent times, and I am a child of those times—the 40s. I can't escape that fact.

The main point of all this is: the conferences were not organized in response to a united appeal for Black conferences on the part of the Black membership of the church. Some had one solution, some had another. But there never would have been Black conferences had it not been for McElhany, Branson, and Nethery and their clear-visioned Black colleagues. They would be fighting still to this day. Now there are more than 190,000 Black Adventists in North America compared to only 17,000 in 1944. The rapid growth of the work among America's largest minority is due in large measure to the strong evangelistic orientation of the regional conferences.

My Ministry

I do not look back on my ministry, which is now more than 40 years, with a lot of sadness, disappointment, heartaches. I have been especially spared and blessed in all the churches I have ministered to and in all the positions or assignments the church has given me. I am blessed that I do not look back on unpleasantness, remembering things—I have to dig far to find them.

I've had disappointments, I've had problems, I've had struggles, but I do not know there have been any great high points. I've been challenged.

I was challenged when the brethren said they were going to ordain me, which meant they were going to affirm me and invest in me the confidence to go out and do ministry on behalf of the whole church. I think that this is a very serious act. It is a great responsibility to be a minister. Ordination is a high moment. When the brethren, representing the people, placed their hands upon me and said, "You are now an ordained minister of this church—a representative of this church," that was great.

I've always found a call to different service or a different area to be a big challenge. To be called to be a departmental director—a minister to ministers, a help to the churches on a conference-wide scale—is a great challenge. I was called to that when I was 26.

Of course, the biggest spots, the high points in one's ministry are the days of baptism when people are born into the kingdom. I've not had a lot of 200- or 300-person baptisms, although sometimes I've had large baptisms. We've had, after a series of meetings and Bible studies, sometimes 5 or 6 people baptized.

Those are great highlights in one's experience. A tremendous satisfaction comes because you know that these people are embarking on a course that will mean a great benefit to them. The third angel's message brings a blessing to every group that it reaches. There is so much potential wrapped up in these people and their children especially, and it is exciting to see them grow. You know when you baptize them that there is going to be growth.

Entering the Ministry

I came to be a minister only gradually. In college I was encouraged by many to be a physician. Dr. Grace Duguid Kimbrough, a protégé of Dr. Kellogg and a prominent physician in Philadelphia, wanted me to go to Temple University or the University of Pennsylvania and on into medicine. She was going to help me with my fees. She had no children of her own, but adopted or raised a couple of children, and was always looking for successors.

When I went to Oakwood, I was thrown in with all kinds of students, some preparing for a profession, and I became convicted concerning the ministry. I began asking the Lord for signs, although I did not know much about signs as such. I was just casting about trying to find out what to do.

There was a certain young woman who was quite unconcerned about spiritual things. I decided that if she went forward during the Week of Prayer and was baptized

MY MINISTRY

and joined the church, that would be a signal for me.

I was 19 or 20 at the time, and I finally decided I wanted to go into the ministry. I was very interested in homiletics and the other courses, and I began reading the lives of preachers like Moody and Spurgeon.

I got a chance to go down to a little church downtown. It was tiny—a little building with a tin roof on Madison and Half Street in Huntsville. After showing myself willing there, the people began to look to me as a sort of ministerial leader. I gave the sermon once or twice and then we had an evangelistic meeting in a community center. Several people joined the church—two or three, maybe four. One of the converts enrolled at Oakwood and later married a conference worker.

So that was a good confirmation and affirmation for me. Sometimes I would visit churches of other faiths in the community, and listen to the ministers preach. I wanted to learn the mind of the people, how they thought, how they responded, how to reach them. So I met several of the ministers and went to their churches. I may even have had the sermon for them once or twice.

Then a Week of Prayer came along. A fine young pastor by the name of W. S. Lee came to Oakwood and spoke. On Sunday, he wanted some assistance because he was going to speak at a large Protestant church in town. I was on the basketball court with several fellows shooting baskets, and he said, "Anybody like to go with me and have the prayer? I've got the service at this church."

I said, "I'll go. I will be glad to go."

On the way back he said to me, "You know, I'd like to have you come down and be the intern in my district." He got in touch with the conference president and with W. W. Fordham, who was the union secretary, and lo and behold! they sent me ministerial internship blanks right away.

They sent me my train fare and I went on out to workers' meeting in Dallas, Texas—a long way in those days. I was still a few hours from graduation. The brethren said, "Well, you only have a few hours to go, you can finish up in the field." And that is what I did.

I went to New Orleans, Louisiana, to be an assistant in the big tent meeting. At that time they gave me supervision of the church in Lake Charles, Louisiana, way on the west coast near Texas. They also gave me the church in Baton Rouge, and the one in Hammond, Louisiana. Besides these they gave me a little company in Covington, Louisiana. I had no automobile, of course, so I got on the train and visited the best I could.

The Lake Charles church was 200 miles from New Orleans. That was a long overnight trip. I would leave New Orleans—we were in the tent meetings, and they went on for weeks—and would go on the train all Friday night to Lake Charles. I would have Sabbath school and church service, get on the train and go back to New Orleans, and be out visiting Sunday morning, rounding up the people to come to the tent.

After the tent meetings, I was placed in Baton Rouge. The district consisted of Baton Rouge, Hammond, and Covington—I did not have to go to Lake Charles anymore. These churches depended on lay leadership; they just didn't have enough pastors to go around. The people were happy I came to Baton Rouge, even though I was only a youngster. I was not married the first two years in the work.

Pastors were few because it was just after the war and also because they were organizing the Southwest Regional Conference. They had to have staff for the new conference, and they assigned the workers in the field to departmental responsibilities.

No Prayer Book

In New Orleans when I would quote someone as if the person was an authority, often a member would say, "Well, his mouth ain't no prayer book!"

That is an old folk saying, and it is deeper than one realizes. People understand and know that so and so is not the final authority. The reference to the prayer book comes from the Catholic background. For them it is authentic. They had many quaint old sayings. Preachers need to listen carefully to the common people. There is wisdom among them.

Early Ministry

Since I was a young preacher, I felt that the church should be a blessing wherever it is. Ellen White compares the church to Ezekiel's river. Wherever it coursed, the land produced rich vegetation. Our people should have an intelligent faith.

I was happy to have a little opportunity for teaching young men in the church who had gifts and abilities. I started a homiletics class, and taught choral conducting.

I also taught just plain reading. Some of the new converts felt that they couldn't take the lead in public services. I would say to one of them, "Now you are going to read the Week of Prayer reading next week" on such and such a night.

"I can't read, Elder."

"Take it and study it. Come back to me. You come back now."

Here I am, only 22 or 23, and the man is 50.

"That's a hard word there. How do you pronounce it?" And we would go over and over, and drill and drill and drill.

Finally, the brother would accept the assignment and do well. In a little while he would be teaching a Sabbath School class, maybe even become an elder.

I've seen our message lift people up. Any given group has people with talent and ability. The pastor must stir up these gifts and bring out the best in his people. Ellen White speaks about the work of God being "retarded by the current unbelief in His power to use the common people to carry forward His work successfully" (*Review and Herald,* July 16, 1895). Clergymen must believe in church members and put responsibility on them. The whole church must be challenged to get into ministry.

New Orleans

In New Orleans many of our church members were very much influenced by the Catholic ethos. They were reverent in church almost to the point of going too far. That influence lessened as you go north in the state. The most southern parts of Louisiana are Creole.

The old Creole deacons did not want the communion table to be uncovered and facing the congregation with the inscription visible on it. They wanted it covered and turned around. They protested like Catholics did after Vatican II, when the priest faced the people and conducted the mass in the vernacular.

So we had a little game. I would turn the communion table around. I wanted people to see this nice table we had bought. The deacons would come and turn it around the other way and cover it. It was a bit humorous. I think they knew what I was doing, but we did not say anything about it.

They also would not allow a woman to clean the rostrum—the platform. Only an ordained deacon could do that. That was the most holy place. Every Sabbath when they came into the sanctuary, they would kneel, have quite a prayer, and get up.

It's nice to have people like that in your church, because they influence others in their decorum. One thing that they had completely unlearned, however, was the custom of making the sign of the cross. In all their great reverence for the house of God I never saw that.

MY MINISTRY

Dixie

I started out in the ministry in southern Louisiana. We used to do Ingathering in places like Bogalusa, a sawmill town. We would even go across the line into Poplarville, Mississippi, Southern Union territory. That part of Louisiana is heavily Catholic. Black people in the United States are traditionally Baptist or Methodist, but in southern Louisiana many are of Catholic background.

This gives them a little different flavor in a way, and even those who are not Catholic are influenced by the culture. Louisiana, you know, still has parishes instead of counties. You hear French phrases spoken. Some of the people speak Creole—Patois. You don't call people godmother or godfather—it's manan and paran. Southwest Louisiana is still Evangeline country. The nickname Cajun comes from Arcadia, the name of the area in Nova Scotia where they came from.

The people had a cute little saying—"lagniappe." When a kid went to the store, he would say to the grocery owner, "Give lagniappe." This could be a licorice stick or a little hard candy—a little something, a trinket, a little gift, a bonus for coming to the store.

I have been told that the term "dixie" also comes out of this area. It derives from the French two dollar piece, a "dieux"—French for "two." That led to "Dixie" for the South.

Northern Louisiana

When I was just a young minister in Baton Rouge, I used to drive through northern Louisiana, the delta area. People, people, people everywhere—especially when you visit on Saturday afternoon. I kept after the brethren and eventually they gave me a little budget and told me to go up there and conduct some meetings.

Elder Samuel Meyers was my associate evangelist. A

gifted preacher and a tremendous musician, he had been highly trained in a Chicago school of music. But he was ashamed by his skills in music—he wanted to be a real man, you know. He could play the piano, the violin, anything. But he didn't want everybody to know.

So we went up and started the meetings. My daughter was an infant in a bassinette—we used to carry her around in it. Sam's second daughter was in a bassinette also. His wife, Gloria, plays the piano, and so does Ethel. They played the piano every night for song service. Bless your heart, those babies never cried once. People would come up after the service and say, "Are you conducting some kind of experiment with these babies? Are they real? What is going on here?"

We had no Black church in Monroe, just a few members in the conference church. The White church was well established, but custom prevented them from being involved in our evangelistic series. When they came to our meetings they had to sit outside—not in the back or around the edges.

These White members were interested in seeing the work established. One of them did the electrical wiring for us. The city fathers were also helpful. They sent a bulldozer to level the lot and bought several loads of sand to improve the drainage. It was the finest tent site I ever had.

The owner of the Buick company, a non-SDA White man by the name of Lennon, asked "Where did you learn the Bible? I studied to be a priest, but I never heard anything like this." And he went on and on.

I did not know who he was until I went to buy a car. He recognized me and called me into his office and said, "Anything you want, let me know." He told his people to clean the car, porcelainize it, fix this and fix that, and put seatbelts on it. "Any time you need something, see me."

After the meetings were over we baptized 35 and organized a little company. The intern coming in had

MY MINISTRY

nowhere to stay. The housing situation was terrible. But the city did have a housing project that had just been built—nothing fancy, a nice clean cinderblock building.

So I went to the car dealer and said, "Mr. Lennon, we have a young preacher coming to town and he has nowhere to stay. What about speaking to the city about a place in the project?"

"Well," he said, "I do not know if I can do anything about that. You have to be in politics, and I have been out of politics for years now."

I said, "You are the only one who can help me. I do not know any other person of your caliber in the city."

The next week he had a nice little apartment for the intern.

Funerals

In New Orleans, funerals were different. The undertakers took care of the minister. They had a special car for him, and only the minister rode in that car. They would come to your home and get you.

The night before the funeral, you had to have the wake. That is a good old Irish custom. The family and friends sit up with the body, but you have to have a little ceremony to open the wake. The minister has a song—usually the only one they knew would be something like "Jesus, Keep Me Near the Cross." After the song he reads a scripture and has a prayer and says, "I now declare the wake open."

I had to learn all about that—no one told me these things at Oakwood College. I was very ill at ease at first, but the senior minister helped me.

The "big" funerals have a band that walks to the cemetery solemnly playing "Nearer My God to Thee" or something like that. When they come back they are not with the family anymore—the family has gone home. Then they play whatever they want.

One of the first funerals I had was for a young girl of 18

who died in childbirth—a young married kid. This was in Covington, and we had no church in the little town. So we got the Baptist church—the biggest in town—and it was packed to the gunwhales. People were sitting in the choir loft and standing.

The people thought you had to show grief by weeping and wailing like the paid mourners in the funerals of Christ's day. They would sob and cry and then they would fall, stiff as a board. At that point I said, "Carry them out . . . carry them out . . . carry them out." I really didn't know what I was doing. But they kept carrying them out. Finally it was time for the eulogy and I got up and said, "You know friends, all of this weeping, crying, and demonstration will not bring this young woman back. Mary is dead. We have to prepare because we are going to follow, and hope that when Jesus comes we will be ready to meet her." I gave them a strong dose of good old Adventist theology on the state of the dead, and the meeting quieted down. They thanked me after the service, and I believe some were influenced for the message.

So I was initiated into the matter of exercising authority. "Now, we are not going to have this," I said. At that time I was only 21! But they quieted down.

Don't Fool With Bradford

In the early days in my ministry I came across ministers of other churches who wanted to fight us. One of them was a Reverend Brown, a great preacher. After I preached several sermons on the Sabbath question, he countered with a sermon arguing that Saturday was a dead day, a Jewish day, and that the Jews were the people who had killed Christ. Against anything Jewish, he was as antisemitic as you can get.

That sermon really stirred the people up, I was told. But Reverend Brown took sick the same night and died the next day. Something had happened to him while he was preaching. The people said, "Don't you fool around with that preacher Bradford. Something may happen to you."

Baton Rouge

The high point of my early years in the ministry came in Baton Rouge, Louisiana. There I helped the little church get its first building.

In spite of not knowing anything about business or building, I learned the meaning of the saying, "A steady stream is better than a cloudburst." I understood even then that to give systematically and regularly is better than a large occasional gift.

The new members were influenced by the custom of their former churches, with their fish fries, bazaars, and so on. I said, "Folks, we don't need to do that. Let's give regularly." W. S. Lee helped me understand that principle. He was my mentor, without my knowing the word.

Founding the little church in Monroe, Louisiana, also gave me great satisfaction. It has lasted through the years and now is a nice-sized congregation.

That is a different country altogether from southern Louisiana. More Protestant, less Creole it has Grambling College there—the college that has developed so many famous athletes, especially in football.

Going into a place without any church you have to take people out of the audience as ushers and helpers. "Will you help take up the offering?" We had some women attending who were willing to help. They worked, as they called it in those days, "in service." That means they were domestic workers. They came at night in their uniforms and looked like uniformed ushers—almost. Some of them were baptized.

A Church of Christ minister fought us tooth and nail. He did everything he could to detract from the meetings. He had a weekly radio program. One night he came and said, "You are preaching false doctrine. I'm going to

THE WIT AND WISDOM OF BRADFORD

challenge you publically when you get on that old Sabbath, and tell the people the truth."

He was threatening me right in the tent after the meeting. His voice was raised and he was agitated. Two of our volunteer women ushers overheard him and interrupting him, said to me, "Reverend, is he bothering you?"

I said, "No."

Finally, when he continued to threaten me, one of them said with her hand in her purse, "Don't worry about him. I have something right here that will take care of him." I do not know what she had—a knife, a gun, or mace. The next Sunday morning he preached on his radio program the usual anti-law, anti-Sabbath sermon. All of us knew it was coming. Every one in town heard it. That night he came to the meeting quite late and couldn't get inside the tent. It was jam-packed, with people out in the street. I gave an illustration of how ministers who fight the law of God are killing themselves. I had seven children with placards to show that the law points out sin, grace, the Saviour, the church, the preacher, et cetera. If there is no law there is no sin, so then we tell the kid with the law to sit down. Of course, if there is no sin you don't need a Saviour, so the kid for that sits down. If there is no Saviour you don't need grace, so that kid sits down. You go through the whole thing until you get to the church, and at last the preacher. Finally the preacher is left and you say, "What are you doing here? You preached yourself out of a job—by condemning the law!"

The people responded enthusiastically. The Church of Christ minister got up and stormed outside. He said, "This fellow must not have heard my sermon this morning." The people sitting nearby laughed at him.

We baptized his church clerk and a couple of others and almost baptized his wife. Later on he became almost friendly and wanted to use some of our equipment.

MY MINISTRY

Those were the days, my friend. We were just youngsters and didn't know it couldn't be done. There was a young convert there who was going into the army and he wanted to be baptized before induction. I said, "OK." We took him to the river—that is the Ouachita River. We didn't test the bottom, and all three of us almost went down—Sam Meyers, this fellow, and myself. It was quite an experience, but we got him through and sent him off to the army and as far as I know he remained faithful to the church.

The Church

On Owning the Church

I love it when a little old lady comes to the General Conference complex and looks around and says, "I'm just looking to see how you are taking care of my property."

The Church

The church is a great fellowship created by the Word. It is people in community. Fosdick once preached a sermon: "Man's Greatest Need Is Community." That is true. We face a fractured world, fractured families, everything fractured, atomized. Yet it is the desire of this atomized society, the more it becomes atomized, to have community. The church satisfies that need. We must make it more satisfying to that need.

The ideal community was on the drawing board for centuries. Poets, seers, and thinkers—people outside the Biblical writers and prophets—longed for community. They wrote about the republic, utopia, the ideal city state.

I believe that is a fundamental longing in man's heart—just as the baby moves toward its mother, no human

THE CHURCH

being is complete without another or at least a significant other.

The church brings people together in Christ. This community created by the Holy Spirit is created by the Word. The Word cuts people out of the quarry of the world and brings them into a sacred fellowship. First of all, they are united with Jesus Christ, and then with each other. That satisfies, or moves toward satisfying, humanity's greatest need.

If the church is not a fellowship, it really isn't anything. The New Testament word is *koinonia*. It can't be just be a group of listeners sitting in a classroom. It can't just be a bunch of spectators at a performance. It's got to be people together in Christ. "Where two or three are gathered in my name, I am there in their midst."

This solidarity of Christian believers is something we need to look at more and more. Adventists are long on proclamation but very short sometimes on genuine community. That is why our people like to hear Scott Peck and others. Anyone who brings community to people will have a hearing, because that is what we all long for. That is why in North America we are talking more and more about relationships. People together in Christ.

We do not just want to be sentimental about this unity. There has to be some anatomy to the body. There has to be a bony structure to hold it together. It cannot be a mass of protoplasm—it must have a form. It must be utilitarian, be useful. The body is for action and for service. It is organized.

There must be authority in this body. Some feel that with my emphasis on the congregation there is a danger of moving the church away from the authority they would like to see in our organization. I reject that. The churches look to each other and as they grow and mature, they recognize that significant other in their brothers and sisters around the world.

Churches have a consciousness, too. I'm talking about congregations. They are not content to be isolated and alone. As one writer says, "We are not saved in splendid isolation." Nor are our churches to be left in splendid isolation. They are to be networked.

Early on the Christian community was networked around the Mediterranean Basin. They sent letters to each other, and they had councils together. They carried the word back from councils so the apostle Paul could say, "As is the experience of all the churches." That is the way it was done in the early church. There was a consciousness that grew out of being one church.

I see the Seventh-day Adventist Church—this movement —as being positioned to reflect that theology with greater clarity than any other body of believers in Christendom. This is because we are a free church, we have thrown off the fetters. We are not tied to the state. This couldn't happen in Europe, because the state churches weren't that free.

Here are, a group of people in the West—in North America, the United States in particular—where a lot of ideas fermented. Here we are looking upon ourselves with a new self-understanding as to what the church really is. Here is the remnant, the people of God gathered out. Organized—"harnessed up" as Israel was for the Exodus.

I do not say that we are the only members of the body of Christ, but we present to the world a visible reality of what the body of Christ is all about. The congregations are networks; there is authority; there is the opportunity for all to confer, to counsel, to make decisions on a worldwide basis.

This, to me, is tremendous. But I come back to the local body. This is the most important, the most vital link because this caring cell gives health to the whole body. The body can have no real health if its cells are impaired, so all our strength and effort must be expended on ministry to and through these local congregations and fellowships and communities—the church that is in this place—because that means health for all places for the church in all places around the world. The growth in grace and strength for service of the local church means health for the whole body. Hence, we have the emphasis on the congregation where we are.

The four great dynamics for church growth and life are the Word, worship, fellowship, and service.

The Word is supreme. Worship is necessary, and fellowship is vital, and service is the result. Through the Word, worship, and fellowship we are being prepared for service. We are challenged, now we are ready. We are harnessed up. We have the armor on. Every member fully instructed and enlightened becomes an outpost in himself or herself of the kingdom of God.

The Church and the Kingdom

We must not mix up the church with the kingdom. That will lead to triumphalism.

The church is interim. The church takes care of the situation between the *already* and the *not yet* . The church can never say in its incomplete form and in its sin—because sin is there—it cannot say, "We are the kingdom." The church can only pray, "Thy kingdom come, thy will be done"—here in our midst, but we are not the kingdom. We are a colony, a part of the church above, but complete membership is never in our hands.

So we must save ourselves from triumphalism and exclusivism. The church is never the possession of human beings. People cannot say, "This is *our* church for *our* kind." Then it becomes a social club, and strangers and outcasts do not feel at home in it. The church must be a home for the homeless. It must be the same as the poet says, "The place where when you come there they have to let you in."

It is never felt that the church is my particular possession, but it is the possession of Jesus Christ. "He is the One who is tenant here," as P. T. Forsythe put it. It is not the church because it has Christ as founder, but it is the church because it has Christ as tenant. It is not apostolic because of a succession of laying on of hands down through history, but it is apostolic because it has internalized, made part of its fabric and its fiber, the apostolic message. It preaches and always goes back to this—not as a creed, but as a living experience. Isn't that a tremendous challenge for the church to reach up to and grasp?

That is what Ellen White meant, I suppose, when she spoke about the church putting on "the panoply of heaven," shining forth into all the world, being a servant to the world, always remembering her sin, always remembering her inadequacies, and always saying to herself, "We need to repent."

Recognizing the nature of sin shows us that we must always repent. Many of our dear folk have sin so catalogued that if they can only avoid committing infraction of the rules they have set for themselves—just like the Pharisees had rules for the Sabbath—they will then be living above sin. We must understand the nature of the law—holy, just, and good—spiritual. Condemning sin and sinfulness.

The church is a place where people say to themselves, "We are sinners," like the alcoholic says, "I am an alcoholic." Everytime I stand in the pulpit, whether I say it in so many words or not, I ought to feel like Paul, "I am the chief of sinners." But, I am a recovering sinner. I am not a deliberately sinning sinner. Jesus has me in intensive care. Only He is able to keep me from falling.

The church is a place where sinners come together and all of them confess to each other from time to time, "I am a sinner. But by the grace of God He is keeping me from day to day. I am not committing known sins. But I know enough about human nature and myself to know that sin remains."

As the old teachers at the Keswick Bible conferences used to say, "Sin remains, but it does not reign." We must never say that it doesn't remain. It is always there. Paul said,

"In my flesh dwelleth no good thing."

The church comes to grips with Romans 7. It learns how to live by the grace of God, learns how to be humble under God, resists the triumphal spirit, and always admits faults and failures, always needing the grace of God.

That kind of church can be forgiving and because it can forgive, it can accept grace. They say that people who can't accept a genuine compliment are usually people who can't give one. So we are not a people deliberately sinning—I have to be careful because some people say that when you preach this kind of theology you are making a cover for sin—but a people who are in recovery, just like recovering alcoholics.

Although I am not deliberately sinning now, although I am not in a consciousness of any infraction of some rule, I do know that I have missed the mark anyway. Even if I have not committed adultery, lied, cheated, stolen, smoked or drank, or whatever, I'm still not full grown as I should be. That is a sin, isn't it? Missing the mark.

It is a marvelous concept that God would take sinners such as we and trust us. He puts us together in fellowship, tells us to learn to live together.

The Perfect Church

The young man comes to Spurgeon and wants to know, "Is your church the perfect church?"

The brother says, "No."

The young man goes away sorrowful like the rich young ruler, with his head down. Then the brother calls him back, "Young man, come back." He says to him, "If you find the perfect church, don't join it—it won't be perfect anymore."

There is always a tendency in us to make a perfect society, utopia. Adventism is afflicted with the utopian ethic. This is why we want to move to the country and so on. That is why we flock to Adventist ghettos as it were.

The ideal community—we love it, we want it, and there's nothing wrong with that longing for it. But to think that human beings can create it is another thing. Because in these communities trouble happens—even in our SDA paradise! Sin crops out even in those enclaves of believers who withdraw from the rest of us and try to isolate and insulate themselves from society.

I think Jesus in His parable of the dragnet and other parables such as those of the wheat and the tares is trying to tell us that you cannot set up a perfect community. That's for the kingdom of God, and God is the one who judges. He is the one who does the separating.

We are to receive everyone as he is. If people have an understanding of the minimum essentials of the gospel, a commitment to being part of the community, and if they love Jesus, we have to accept them. We cannot cleanse the church by our own zeal.

Ellen White said it would cause great havoc if we allowed our plans to get away with us and we began cutting off and purging, cleansing as we wanted to. There would be awful hurt, and there has been through the years.

The Church

What it isn't: a monarchy ruled by humans.

What it is: a group of servant leaders who understand the nature of this body.

In Ephesians 4:11-16 we're into anatomy—structure, organization. But there is more than anatomy here. We're into physiology also. How the body works. The dynamics of the system. The church is not static. It is growing, powerful. This happens when each part does its work. Look at the text carefully. Preach it. Teach it. This is the text for the 90s.

The North American Division

The North American Division

We still have troubles in North America about who is going to do what. North America has been almost a proving ground for General Conference programs, since there was no North American Division as such for so long. In 1912 or 1913 there was a formal organization of the North American Division conference. But that was a disaster because it destroyed the very genius of our organization—that is the GC is a joining of all its subsidiary organizations. All come together in the GC. Divisions are all part of the General Conference. The union is the highest constitutional body, the unit on which the General Conference rests.

The General Conference does not rest on its divisions; it works through its divisions. In North America as we have tried to bring some identity and power to act, to do on behalf of the General Conference for North America, there have been some situations where we have run into each other.

I often give the illustration of a lawn to be mowed. The General Conference tells its divisions what to do and where to work—it defines the territory and gives an assignment. It says to the North American team, "You mow this lawn here. This is your territory." But often there are those who have been mowing here all the time and they cannot understand the new reality. So when we go out to mow the lawn, we find several out there mowing the lawn. We may want to mow diagonally, like my gardener does. Some may want to mow it straight. There we are, all of us, trying to mow the same lawn. It is a pretty difficult situation and no one is really in charge of mowing the lawn. But more and more we are learning to work together. Our assignments and terms of reference are becoming clearer.

A Little Authority

We have two sons, and when we moved here, each of them finally had their own room. Earlier on, they had both stayed in the same room, but when they got to be big boys we were glad to have several bedrooms so we could give each one a room. We assigned each boy a room and of course our daughter also had her room.

Ethel told the kids, "You take care of your room. You can put up posters or whatever you wish, but you keep the room clean." She gave them their assignment and put them on their own. Even when she wanted to reprimand them, and it was our home—we were paying the mortgage—we respected our children's little place. We would knock before we went in the room.

Now, it was our home, and the boys were our sons, but they had their own room. We had given them this room. We wanted that little spot to be theirs.

That is the way we approach North America. The brethren have given us an assignment. This is, as it were, the room where they want us to work, and we have pled for the privilege of a little authority in this room.

Preaching

Adventist Preaching

I am interested in preaching. I have read everything Ellen White ever said about preaching, I think. Perhaps the greatest statement that I could find is in Evangelism around page 500, where she says that people aren't longing for even prayer or music, but longing for the Word to hear it just as it reads.

If the church is going to be strong, if we are going to grow up as a church, then we are going to have to take seriously what Jesus meant when He said, "Feed my lambs and my sheep." Feeding is not only as in quartering the horses and the cattle and giving them their hay, but feeding as in training and guiding. The people must be prepared for service, to act as responsible members of Christ's body. Preaching is basic, fundamental. It is a part of ministry and should serve to prepare a people for the coming of the Lord.

You can say "I am going to preach as Jesus did," and just sit on a nice rock and speak to the people in conversational tones. None of this raising the voice and getting excited. But to just sit and talk to them in a nice folksy way wouldn't go down very well where I started in the ministry. The people had seen big revival meetings come through.

THE WIT AND WISDOM OF BRADFORD

Those were the last days of the big tent campaigns. Billy Graham was just coming into his own, and so was Oral Roberts. The message had to be given in clear clarion tones. None of this pianissimo-whispering hope, as Earl Cleveland calls it.

Seventh-day Adventists had to make an impression on the community, we had to get their attention. So we had to preach, proclaim. Maybe we were a little theatrical, but I would hope that we are not being judged too harshly for this.

In those days we gave attention to prophetic/doctrinal preaching more than we do now. We gave a steady diet of doctrine and prophecy. We went over the fundamentals again and again. It was heavy, concentrated. The people reeled under it, and there was a reaction. People said: "Look at my life's situation, where I am living today, the real world. I must do more than just remember the 27 fundamentals, the 2300 days. I need something more than to hear them expounded every Sabbath, to sustain my spiritual life. I need something more. I have to meet people, I have to meet real life situations. I am involved in all of this thing called life."

So we began to develop a better educated clergy. We had a seminary coming along. In my early days there was an advanced Bible school—they called it the seminary, but it was just getting underway.

Then there were those who said we had to be concerned about people. More people oriented. Often that took a psychological turn. Maybe Harry Emerson Fosdick influenced us too much—he was the life situation preacher. And, of course, at the same time there was Norman Vincent Peale's positive thinking. We now have the gospel of wealth and blessing, of affluence, of belief in one's self—self-esteem, et cetera. We have them all the way from the Reverend Ike to Robert Schuller.

There was good in this, but as most human beings do,

Grandfather Robert L. Bradford was a first-generation SDA minister.

Charles, as a boy, with his parents, Robert (a second-generation SDA minister) and Etta.

Sister Myrna Bradford

Sister Lucille Douglas

Sister Eva and husband George Rock

Brother Terrence Milton Bradford

Sister Vera and husband George Braxton

The adult Bradford children in 1987: Charles, Sharon, and Dwight

The Bradford family, 1967, l to r: Dwight Lyman; Charles Edward, Jr.; CEB; Ethel; Sharon Louise

Daughter Sharon and son-in-law James Lewis

Grandchildren Marquita and Jay

A letter from my dad . . .

1216 Idlewood Ave.
2-7-46
Richmond, Va.

Dear Chas;-

Glad to hear from you. Glad you are doing nicely. Keep up the good work.

This leaves me as well as usual by God's help. Hope you are doing well.

Am a very busy man still. Getting 12 people ready for baptism next month.

The girls in Phila. were quite disappointed you did not make the trip there during the holidays. Am quite sure you know by now. All the family is well as far as I know.

Find enclosed check for $25.00. Buy shoes and books. Use the rest for what ever you need only be discrete. Glad you received money for exams in time.

I am trying to get a tent for the summer. If I do I can use you as a tent master, and Bible teacher. Chances are good for a tent. The opportunities are very good. As good as I ever saw.

If this does not materialize, I will be glad to have you in Petersburg. It would be a great help for I am overworked very much.

My district is right up there among the leaders. God is good to me. I hope to not fail Him.

What kind of work are you doing now? Sorry you could not get on with Carter. I suppose you needed a rest anyhow. You have hit it strigent for quite a spell. You are to be commended.

My greatest human draw back is not having your mother with me to help out as no one but she knew how too. I miss her very much. But the good Lord knows what is best. Let us be ready to meet her in the first resurection.

Times are critical. The world is facing famine. This country is being called on to share with the folks in Europe. Revolution in the U.S. is just around the corner. This strike at nation is a veritable forerunner of revolution. U.N.O. is already doomns. What does it all mean? The end of all things is at hand. Amos 4:12 is the warning.

Well son, I must close. Pray for me and I will pray for you. I am
    Yours.
      Dad.

Elder Bradford is pictured here with the church officers of the Baton Rouge, Louisiana, church, which was his first pastorate.

Press release following election of Elder Bradford as the first Black man to hold the post of North American Division president. (1979)

Pictures of Elder Bradford with two presidents of the United States. He presented each president a set of the *Bible Story* books.

Pictured are persons baptized and the crusade team in the St. Louis Berean church, 1953.

Elder Bradford was honored by the Greater Washington, D.C., Oakwood College Alumni Association in 1987.

PREACHING

we swung the pendulum or the swinging door too far—an either/or mentality. We felt if we were going to get into life situations, the preaching and counseling type thing, we had to abandon completely the doctrinal/prophetic emphasis.

I think we lost our frame of reference. We Seventh-day Adventists must know who we are to preach effectively to the times and the people living in these times. We must know who we are. There must be no identity crisis. Role models have to be chosen carefully, and the model for Adventist preaching is still the herald proclaiming the good news and the glad tidings. Seventh-day Adventists are here to call attention to the things that count, that matter. What is ultimate? The theological world is coming back to eschatology and apocalyptic which Kasemann said is the mother of theology. This is the "soul" of Adventism.

So we don't want to leave off prophetic doctrinal preaching, but neither do we want to swing again so far as to forget human need—the people in the pew, where they are.

I think we are swinging back to balance. We are producing some fine young theologians today. Their heads are in the right place and they are going after prophecy, after good solid Bible study. Bible study is back in vogue. People are studying the Word, preachers are studying the Word. Now we have to learn how to communicate it better.

But whatever the style, preaching must have content—substance. Isn't this what one of the great English writers said to the young man who thought that he had written the perfect novel. "Young man, your manuscript has style but no substance.

And while I am in this vein, I think it was George Bernard Shaw who said about a certain playwright's script, "It is both original and good. Unfortunately the good part is not original, and the original part is not good."

THE WIT AND WISDOM OF BRADFORD

Encourage the Preacher

I don't think there is any better preaching today than Adventist preaching. We have a lot of folks that go out and hear one or two sermons and take a one-person poll and say that the preaching in the church today is terrible. I don't go along with that.

So instead of knocking those who are trying to be effective speakers and preachers, effective messengers and servants of the Word, we need to support these people and talk them up. Praise them (in the right way), pat them on the head and say, "Brother, you are doing a great work and we appreciate you." This is what the church needs.

We who are on committees and boards, who are appointing ministers and planning for the training of ministers, should be saying, not only by a few pronouncements but by our very actions, that we think good solid preaching is important to the church. The enrichment and strengthening of pastoral ministry is where it's at. This is where the battle is won.

I say at the risk of sounding mercenary or crass, the "biggest bang for the buck"—the greatest impact to the church—is the tithe dollar. Out of every dollar out there in the field given by dear little Sister Mary Jane or whoever, 20 cents winds up at the General Conference. This is immediate. Enlightened self-interest would dictate that the strengthening of that person in the pulpit who brings the people together for the study of the Word, worship, fellowship, and service, is helpful to all of us. He is the one putting corn in the crib. The Bible says not to muzzle the ox that treads out the corn.

So I am for heightening, raising up, honoring the pulpit. Not in the way to make a great star out of anyone, or to make some great superstar, but for enriching the whole pastoral ministry. The pastoral ministry is where it is at, and the sharing of the Word of God is the most important activity in the Adventist church. To learn to do it well, is to serve the cause of God.

Emphasis on Pastoral Ministries

Ministry, which in the New Testament sense is service, belongs to the whole church. A ministry is given to the whole people of God. The entire church becomes Christ's servant and is accordingly given its function, purpose, and structure—which is essentially missionary. The total community is responsible for a ministry to and for the world.

But there are special ministries given to the church which enable it to carry out the mission of God in the world. These special ministries are so bound up with the church's mission and her ability to perform it that it is possible to say that they are representative of the whole. These servants who equip, inspire and facilitate "are as great or as small as their effectiveness in making every church member, including the smallest and most despised, an evangelist in his own home and environment" (*Anchor Bible,* Vol. 34A, pp. 379, 380).

It becomes therefore the task of the community of faith to strengthen and enhance the ministry of these servants of God's servants. The persons given this special ministry become symbolic of that ministry which is entrusted to the whole church.

"The gift of the exalted Christ to the church consists, according to Ephesians, of persons. Unless the church respects the men and women given her, she does not revere her head, Christ . . . All the ministers listed (apostles, prophets, evangelists, pastors who teach) are persons who fulfill their service by speaking: they are 'Ministers of the word' " (*ibid.,* p. 436).

The building up of the body of Christ, the church, depends upon the efficiency and power of those persons with special ministries. When these pastors, for that is precisely what they all are, understand their function and willingly give all their strengths and gifts to the performance of it the whole church becomes equipped for service.

"God's ministers are symbolized by the seven stars which He who is the first and the last has under His special care and protection. The sweet influences that are to be abundant in the church are bound up with those ministers of God, who are to represent the love of Christ . . .

"It is to the honor of Christ that He makes His ministers a greater blessing to the church, thru the working of the Holy Spirit, than are the stars to the world" (*Gospel Workers,* pp. 13, 14).

As these persons exercise their charisma Messiah's body develops; unifying intelligent faith reproduces in the community the image of the perfect standard—the Pattern Man. Individual members become "no longer babes tossed by waves and whirled about by every doctrinal gust, (and caught) in the trickery of men who are experts in deceitful scheming" (Eph. 4:14). They become effective ministers of the word on their own "speaking the truth in love," a serving, caring, growing community.

Suggestions for Young Preachers

Young preachers have to read. How readest thou? A good reading program is absolutely necessary. I'm preaching things that I may not have seen before because I am reading more widely. I've tried in my feeble way to follow what I have taught in homiletics classes and especially as conference president.

Unless young preachers are into reading and the program of study that challenges and stretches their minds, they are not going anywhere. The mind stretched by great concepts or ideas never comes back to its original shape. It is stretched. So we have to stretch ourselves. Young preachers have to learn to pick out from here and there, to have eyes to see.

H. M. S. Richards tells this one, "The cattleman said

PREACHING

'that the preacher has hoof and mouth disease. [I notice preachers never laugh when I tell this story in their midst. It must hit home to us too closely.] He can't preach and doesn't visit.' " Then Richards added, "It's because he doesn't visit that he can't preach."

My friend Charles Dudley says, "A house-going preacher makes a church-going people." So we learn to preach in the homes of the people. Some of these people who are into psychological preaching are doing it from a book, or from a theory they have gotten from Erickson, or Fromm, or Freud, or maybe even Menninger, my favorite along that line. But to know the needs of people is to be with them, to live amongst them.

The preacher is chosen from among the people. He must never leave the people. The Lord in His earthly journey was of us, a part of us, with us, pitched His tent by our tent, and the preacher has to do it too. He has to identify with the people. He has to live with them. He has to know them. He has to understand them. He has to know their language, to rap with them, to communicate with them. He has to feel what they feel. That is absolutely *sine qua non*—you can't preach unless you know the people.

You can give great orations, you can scintillate and know persuasion techniques and everything else such as setting the mood or the ambience of the place, but you can never be able to continue in ministry based on that. The only effective continuing ministry has to be authentically based in the Word of God and in the people's lives.

So you have a preaching arc, a hermeneutical arc. The Bible is over here at one end, and the people and their needs over there. Real preaching joins and connects the two. Ellen White says the Bible and the soul of man were made one for the other. So we have to bring vital doctrines in contact or connection with the heart, the soul, the needs of people, enriching their lives. There is a kind of synergism here. That is real preaching.

We have to give attention in this church to preaching. We need to see more about it in our journals, in the *Ministry* magazine and even in the good old *Review*. We have to tell the people: "You, too, are part of the preaching." P. T. Forsythe says, "Preaching is the ordered hallelujah of the witnessing community." That is what preaching is—not a monologue, but dialogue. It is interaction.

People need to be trained to respond to the preaching. Now some churches are criticized for being too charismatic, too loud, too noisy. That is inappropriate. That is not what I am talking about. I am talking about interaction. My wife and I can interact without saying a word, we have been together for so long. So the people, the deacons, the elders must be challenged to greater sensitivity and empathy. They must look on preaching also as encounter with principalities and powers, and all of us can have our part in the conflict.

The people must know what is happening in the preaching event. They must know also that their involvement, their prayers, their response has much to do with the outcome.

Intelligent, involved congregations would neutralize the power of the enemy and make the ministry of the world a thousandfold more effective. When Adventism is characterized by such congregations, the church militant will become the church triumphant.

On Sermon Preparation

I love to read about John Jasper. He was a slave, but finally he became one of the most celebrated clergyman of his day. All classes of people came from all over to hear him preach. He was a tremendous preacher although he was almost illiterate—which is not the same as being ignorant. He would tell the story of his conversion. His mother was praying for him as he worked in the tobacco factory. She had a friend who worked next to him at the factory who was a Christian and she asked him to pray for John. So they prayed together.

Well, it so happened that John became burdened with his sins. And as they would say in those days, finally he "gave in to the Lord." He thought he would quietly tell his fellow worker who was also his mother's prayer partner, "I's come through." But it came out as a roaring shout. He put his hand over his mouth to try to hold it in, but when he repeated it, it came out again even louder.

The boss heard the commotion, came down on the floor, and said, "What is the matter? What's going on here?"

The old praying partner said, "John Jasper, John's got religion!"

Instead of the boss popping the whip on them he said, "Stop the wheels and let him tell it."

And old John said, "I's been telling it ever since."

He organized and was pastor of the sixth Mount Zion church in Richmond, Virginia. His fame spread, and the big boys from the seminaries and fashionable churches came to see him. The streets were jammed with horses and carriages on a Sunday afternoon when he preached at churches other than his own. "John, how do you do it?" his visitors asked. "How do you prepare your sermons?"

"Well, I reads myself full. Then I go down to the St. James River and I walk it in. Then I prays myself warm. Then I go to the pulpit and I preach it out." You can't find a better formula.

Black Preaching

I've been reading a book by David Buttrick of Vanderbilt University entitled Homiletics. In it he says that the best preaching going on today is in the Black church, because Black preachers preach to a picture. The most effective preaching that I've ever done is when I was involved myself and a part of a picture, when it was vividly etched on my mind.

The authentic Black preaching fathers had a vivid imagination. The genre is dying out now. But those older men could preach to a picture so effectively. They would probably fail the test in doctrinal preaching and to articulate how they did what they did by some homiletical rules would put them at a great loss. But they were widely read.

This is narrative and descriptive type preaching. Buttrick and others say that this is really New Testament preaching, what Jesus did. He went about doing good, He healed the sick, and so forth, and with many other words He exhorted the people. New Testament preaching describes the event. Brunner tried bringing in something like that by talking about event, encounter, what's happening now. Even old Bultmann said that something ought to be happening in the pulpit, that something ought to be created right there. The Word of God should come alive right there again.

When it comes to the narrative part of it, one could not excel these men with their wonderful God-given imagination. But they were horribly off doctrinally and some of them were not even living worthy lives, although many of them were godly men. They steeped themselves in Scripture. They lived in it, they were with it.

D. T. Niles says, "From time to time the preacher is privileged to enter into the Biblical conversation." The conversation becomes relevant when he is able to get into it. Exegesis is the aperture through which we can get into it. I don't think we can do any real authentic preaching until we have done our work on the text and been admitted into what's happening in the Biblical world.

But SDA preaching must go beyond all this. We have, within the larger Christian community, a teaching ministry —line upon line, precept upon precept, etc. We have to set the record straight. Our focus must be on preparing a people to be evangelists and teachers of righteousness in their own right to the nations—to the whole world.

Preparing to Preach

I would have been a much better preacher if I had had to stay with a congregation for 10 years. I am a guest preacher now, and we guest preachers are prone to take our nice hobbyhorses and go out and do wonderfully. That is not a great test, however.

The best I can do is put myself in imagination with the dear people I am going to preach to. Menninger said, "In your congregation if you have 100 people you are going to have this problem here, this one, this one, 5 percent of the people struggling with this, some have suicide in their family, some will have had a death, and so on." The least I can do is try to establish some kind of empathy for those people. So I am thinking of the people as I prepare.

I'm reading. I'm studying all the time, making a few notes here and there. As I read I make my own index in the back of the book. My mind is working. We learn from the psychologists and psychiatrists that the mind is never in neutral. All these ideas are there. So we think about the people and want to minister to them. The events of the day, things we have read, our prayer life, and out of all this something comes out. I hear someone say something in a sermon and I think, *That is good for the people.* I write it down, develop it, and make it my own.

Now of course, as in life, most beginnings do not see the light of day. We have to keep a lot of them going. There ought to be some way we can keep a little record of what we have thought. At night we might wake up, and we need to write things down.

In the Black church when a brother brings you up to speak and introduces you to the congregation, he may say something like, "Now, Brother _____ will come before us in his own way." That is a beautiful statement! "In his own way"—he's not going to come as Vandeman, or Ron Halverson, or E. E. Cleveland, or C. D. Brooks, but he's going to come in his own way. Now he has learned from all of them. He's learned from everybody that he has contacted and touched or who has touched him, but he is going to come in his own way. The Word of the Lord is going to come through him.

Preaching is sharing ourselves. It's a testimony.

But it's not testimony apart from Scripture. This is the original witness—Scripture. Calvin talked about the testimonium, that in me which harmonizes with Scripture. My experience in Christ now is validated by and rooted in Scripture, and testifies to Scripture.

I don't like only witnessing and testimony, because sometimes they are not authentic, not based on Scriptural realities. Too subjective. They tend toward sensationalism and become shallow. Ellen White talked about some who were good exhorters, but she says it takes a little more than being able to exhort in order to lead the congregation, the people in their pilgrimage—their journey from this world to the next.

Is this what Paul is talking about when he says, "Therefore let us leave the elementary teachings about Christ and go on to maturity, not laying again the foundation of repentance from acts that lead to death, and of faith in God, instruction about baptisms, the laying on of hands, the resurrection of the dead, and eternal judgment. And God permitting, we will do so" (Heb. 6:1-3, NIV)?

Preaching Models

I have been influenced in preaching to a great extent, first of all by my father's friends.

I was not with my own father during his ministry, and when I was old enough to really get into it I wasn't interested in ministry. When I left home to go to school he was not pastoring large churches because he was retired. I

PREACHING

was told by many that he was a tremendous Bible expositor, a teacher-type preacher.

I was influenced by some of the older evangelists. I sat under Elder George E. Peters who was the pastor of the Ephesus Church in New York City. That was after the Humphrey schism. He rented a big church on Lennox Avenue and gathered the people together.

Peters was a tremendous evangelist. His forte was in calling people to accept Christ. He labored with them. Some may say he overdid it, but it was excusable in a man who was so intense in his search.

I was influenced also by Elder T. M. Rowe. He was the pastor in Philadelphia when we were there. My dad was coming back to the ministry then, recovering. He would take care of a couple of the little churches up in Pennsylvania, but to be with the kids I was mostly there in Philadelphia.

Rowe was a prince of preachers. He was tall and thin. He had had his kneecaps broken when he was out doing Ingathering on the ice. So he walked with a little different step—he had to lift his foot in a certain way. All these things a kid would notice. Rowe believed in developing the worship service, and in good preaching and good singing. He was not the traditional doctrinal Adventist preacher, because he read widely from other Protestant literature. He was good at bringing that in. He had a certain way, certain mannerisms that were unforgettable, the inflection of his voice, and so forth.

Among friends that I have known that are not Seventh-day Adventists, the man who has had the greatest influence is Gardner Calvin Taylor. He is the pastor of the Concord Baptist Church in Brooklyn, New York.

I knew Gardner when he was a young fellow in Baton Rouge, Louisiana, and this big Concord Church in Brooklyn became vacant. The large Black churches would consult people like Benjamin Mayes or Mordecai Johnson on pastoral assignments. I think it was Mayes or someone who said, "That young fellow Taylor, get him up to preach." After he preached to them, that was it. He has been there ever since, since the 1950s and is going to retire soon.

He is the most eloquent man I have ever heard in the pulpit, a tremendous preacher. His dad before him was a preacher. He is a different cut from most of them. He respects Adventists a great deal, and he keeps in touch with me every now and then. I go to hear him speak. I have also preached for him. He has a congregation of 12,000 people, but they don't all come every Sunday.

The church burned down when he first went there as a young pastor. He had to rebuild it and now it's a marvelous preaching auditorium with a tremendous order of service. They know how to worship at that church. Taylor is widely sought after for lectures, et cetera. He's a highly educated man, and everybody in Protestantism knows him. He's not your fundamentalist man, however. He likes Billy Graham and they are friends, but he doesn't believe that Graham preaches to the people's needs.

He, of course, has been affected by his peers in ministry who are top men. In fact, some of the professors from Union Theological Seminary used to hold membership in his church. One was Saunders, the great New Testament scholar. Mrs. Roosevelt used to attend his church also.

He is such a kind, gracious man, and a man of great knowledge. He went over big in Australia: they made him preach all day and night while he was there some years ago.

He can do something with a text like a lot of Black Baptist ministers. He once gave a talk in Boston that was a masterpiece. The occasion was the death of Martin Luther King or some big event like that. He went to the Book of Luke where Luke brings in the birth of Christ in such and such a year, and Taylor said that in a certain year of [a

PREACHING

president] that such and such came and the Word of the Lord came to Martin Luther King.

My favorite sermon is the last one that did pretty well. We preachers know that we live for this moment, that the next one is not promised to us. Sometimes, as Spurgeon said, the chariot wheels drag heavily. Yes, even Spurgeon had his moments—he said that sometimes the ashes almost get cold on the altar. It's because we're all human, because God's message is filtered through this humanity of ours.

That's why the hearers must have the Holy Spirit with them. Some of what we say needs to be, at least, if not filtered, modified a bit. The Holy Spirit needs to take it and apply those parts of it that are pure winnowed wheat.

The gospel always comes through earthen vessels.

I should tell you how I received a ministerial license at age 19. I was working with Frank L. Bland as tentmaster in Philadelphia, Pennsylvania. He was a tall, big-framed man, very impressive, but quite young to be pastor of the Ebenezer church. My mother called him her boy.

Frank and his wife, Olga (they called her the songbird of the South—she was really the Marian Anderson of our church), took a real interest in me. He asked me to be his tentmaster when I was just 19 years old. It was during the war. I hadn't as yet received my 4D which was the classification for ministerial students. J. L. Morand, the Oakwood College president, warned us "If you don't have a 4D you must stay at Oakwood and work on the farm in the summer." But I was getting my head into ministry and wanted to get some experience. So I accepted Elder Bland's offer to join him in summer evangelism.

But before the meetings started I received a notice from the Draft Board. I must come down for an examination and preparation for induction. I went to F. L. and he said, "Don't worry. I'll speak to the conference about this" (meaning the East Pennsylvania Conference). Imagine my surprise when during the campmeeting the conference president called me in and told me that the conference committee had granted me a ministerial license and although I had gone through the pre-induction physical, the 4D classification came through, and I was able to return to college in the fall and never had to do military service. Some of my friends were surprised to see me back at school in the fall.

I must add something about W. W. Fordham, W. S. Lee, and F. L. Bland. These are the three men who had most to do with my early ministry. I won't be able to live with these brethren and their families if something isn't said here.

W. W. Fordham and W. S. Lee were "my main men." They were young, bold, tremendous role models. Successful evangelists. W. S. Lee was my first supervising pastor. He took care of business, paid attention to detail, and didn't mind telling me or any intern that worked with him just how they were doing.

I left Oakwood to help him in a big tent meeting in New Orleans in 1946. I was impressed with his library, his wide reading. W. S. was no-nonsense, intense in what he did. But he and his wife took me in as a little brother. Every intern needs such a mentor to get his feet on the ground and to understand the realities of ministry.

All of the above have influenced me personally, but the one preacher who has shaped my generation of preachers above all the rest is E. E. Cleveland. Not only through his speaking ability, but also by his deep commitment to public evangelism. His singleness of purpose. His determination to spread Adventism.

The church owes Earl a debt of love for he kept the fires burning.

He has experienced more than 10,000 baptisms during a span of 45 years, most in the great cities of North America. He made himself a good writer, read himself into theological competing, and preached until he became one

PREACHING

of the greatest communicators, bar none. And he never stayed too long with a single method. The game never passed him by. Earl Cleveland always stayed ahead. Even in semi-retirement he conducts old-fashioned tent meetings lasting 4-6 weeks and resulting in 100-150 baptisms.

He has to lead the list.

The Ministry

The Meaning of Ministry

They say that a Catholic is brought up expecting the high moment of his life when he says his first mass. That is the acme—the zenith, the great moment.

A Protestant boy grows up, and his great moment comes when he takes the pulpit and preaches.

Both of these boys may have had their eyes on the wrong moment. As the old English preacher said, "After the meeting, the service begins."

If someone comes up to the church and asks, "Is the service done?" (that is the way they speak in England), the old brother says, "No, the meeeting is over, but the service has not yet begun."

That is the essence of ministry—service. But it does not dawn on us all at once, because we come up through a school system and through a church system where the sermon is the great thing, or the service of worship, or administrative duty.

It's like the old preacher who prayed, "Lord, use me, especially in an administrative capacity." We all have some of that.

What is ministry really all about? Someone said, "After

THE MINISTRY

the shouting and the hurrahs, the great sermon is still an affront to God and a curse to man unless genuine ministry results."

There was the preacher who had given what he thought was a very great sermon. As he and his wife were walking home to the manse, he said to her, "You know, there are very few great preachers in the world."

She said, "And one less than you think, my dear."

When a truly great preacher gave a sermon that everybody was complimenting him about, he said, "The devil has told me that already."

Now, the devil would want us to believe that ministry is some spectacular experience or performance. But we will have to look to the Jesus model. That model is service.

I read in Matthew 20 where the mother brings her sons and wants the Master to put one of them on each side of Him. He told her that the Gentiles exercised that kind of authority and power. They told people where to go, where to stand. But, in His kingdom it will not be like that. If you want to be great in the kingdom, you must be a servant. Then He points to Himself as a role model and says, "I did not come to be served, but I came to serve. And that is the way it must be in My kingdom."

As you continue to reflect on this, you say to yourself, "Why didn't Paul use some other words to describe ministry?" He used the word for deacon, and he keeps on using it. He doesn't use any words that suggest hierarchy or clericalism, but only ministry.

The pastor must epitomize the ministry of the church. Above all people, he should understand what ministry is about. He should not be swayed by other considerations.

That is a heavy, heavy load. It is a heavy obligation, a difficult rule to live by. Because we are all human—we all want to be approved. We all want to be loved, appreciated, and affirmed, and we need that. We want to be scratched. So we have to keep telling ourselves that the real ministry

THE WIT AND WISDOM OF BRADFORD

we bring to the church is in service.

So every gift—preaching, teaching, administration, guidance—whatever it is, no matter how brilliant, how scintillating, must be brought to the feet of Jesus and must be employed in the service of the community.

The *Anchor Bible* translates Matthew 20 this way: "He gave Himself for the community." The one who is a minister gives himself for the service of the community, to build up the community.

We ought to build up the community as Paul says, not with wood, hay, and stubble, but with precious metal and precious stones that will last. We must do good, solid work so that it will stand.

I heard one pastor say, "Man, when I left that church, it fell to pieces."

I said, "What did you put it together with? You were there for four or five years. Why did it fall to pieces?"

Ministry is bringing out the best in people. It means bringing out their gifts, employing these gifts and skills. It means seeing people better off and more equipped to serve when we leave a parish than when we go to the parish.

Once my dad was at a big meeting in Chicago, at the Shiloh Church. It was a big church even in his day. Several brethren got up and said, "When I came to Chicago there wasn't a thing here." Another said, "When I came to Chicago, there wasn't anything here." Three men got up and said the same thing. We need to express more freely sincere appreciation for the work our colleagues in ministry have done. Rule #1—Praise your predecessors.

Well, I do not think we should disregard what others have done, because we are laying on the same foundation. I do feel we ought to leave it stronger and more seaworthy than when we came. Otherwise our ministry has been an entertainment. It has been a babysitting thing and not really a soul-building, soul-strengthening, experience-stretching thing where people become more and more fulfilled.

THE MINISTRY

This may sound too theoretical and too optimistic, but we still have to aim at it. We are always failing, but we are getting up and trying again that our ministry might be what God would have it to be.

Advice to Young Ministers

To someone just starting out in the ministry I would say: live with the people. Get to know people's psyche, their minds. You must be able to communicate with the people.

I grew up in a strong Adventist culture that was aloof from society, almost a ghetto. My parents were somewhat older when I came along. My father was a strong disciplinarian and my mother very sweet. I had not lived in circumstances like the South. I almost thought I was better than the people there. Even our speech patterns were different. For all practical purposes I was an outside missionary coming into a foreign culture.

I decided to learn the people and become one of them. I did not know that people in some parts of the country spoke to everybody in the street. In New York and Philadelphia you do not speak to people because you never know what might happen. Everybody is out to get you. People walked fast and looked straight ahead. Nobody talks to strangers. Anonymity is highly prized.

You can understand how a young, shy preacher could be misunderstood as being proud, withdrawn, feeling better than others, etc.

Early I knew I had better learn how to relate to these people. I had better learn their speech, rap with them, understand them. So I would go to other churches and community gatherings, and after awhile I could identify with them. I felt comfortable and good being with people.

No matter what degree a person has—theology, psychology, sociology—he had better get down with the people.

One day a highly educated pastor became frustrated over his sermons. They seemed to float straight over the heads of his listeners and out the door. In desperation he cried, "O Lord, where are you?"

Whereupon the Lord said: "I'm down here with the people."

They make fun of some of us preachers, saying that we are six days invisible and on the seventh incomprehensible. But like Jesus we must understand the people. "The common people heard Him gladly." We must be able to do as Wesley said—"Plain talk." Wesley preached his sermon to his charwoman. If she could understand it, he would take it out to the public. But if she didn't, he would rework it or scrap it. It was a strain for Wesley because he was an Oxford don, a brilliant man.

That is my advice to young preachers and teachers and workers: you've got to be with the people.

I'm getting to the place that I feel I can rap with any people, anywhere. You know what I mean? I can kid with them, I can laugh with them, I can meet with them, and I can rejoice with them, and when the time comes I can give them a little word of admonition and they will accept it. They feel that I am one of them, identifying with them.

This is something we have to consciously do and not allow this beautiful Advent message to separate us instead of making us a part of the people. The acid test is to take great truths and make them simple—to take the deep truths of salvation and make them intelligible to people in the pew. To make the vision so plain that the person running by can read and understand.

The Priestly Order

We do have deposits of a priestly idea of ministry that have been left among us. This residual is because we are all brought up with too much of the magical and mysterious attached to ministry. Theologians call it sacerdotal—having

THE MINISTRY

to do with priestly ministration.

For instance when I was a boy, you couldn't go into the rostrum—that was a sin. Some called it the Most Holy Place. They didn't come out and say it often, but that was the thought.

I cannot see where the New Testament uses any of the thought forms, the ideas, the concepts of priesthood and applies them to ministers—to human ministers, servants. All of these priestly terms apply to Jesus Christ.

If we as Seventh-day Adventists rightly understand the types and symbols of the Old Testament and the sanctuary, we will have to say that none of them apply to us, making us priests. All apply to Jesus Christ. The human priest was only a type of Christ.

We must be careful not to apply the same kind of symbolism and typology that applied to the priesthood in the Old Testament to a group of human beings. All priesthood is swallowed up in Jesus Christ. As one translation said, "It [the earthly priesthood] became senile, obsolete, and passes away."

So we have a new ministry. We have also the New Testament teaching of the priesthood of the believers.

Does that mean that everyone is immediately a pastor? No. In the New Testament church, the Holy Spirit selects the pastors. He programs them, as it were. Not altogether in some mysterious way, as sometimes we have thought, but by giving them gifts and the call. These gifts, and natural skills, with the outpouring of the Holy Spirit upon them, equip people to serve in various areas and in many ways to the church.

I think it is a bit much when we look upon ourselves individually as priests, mediators between God and the people. There is only one mediator between God and man—the man Jesus Christ. We must not observe His priestly ministry. Pastors are servants of God's servants. But they are by no means saviors of the people. If we regard ordination to ministry as exhaltation to priestly status, we come close to identifying with the falling away under which human beings arrogated to themselves the perogatives of Christ's priestly authority and ministry. "Purge out the old leaven!"

We are—all of us, preachers and people—servants. We need each other. We must help each other. The whole congregation—under God—becomes a praying, witnessing, ministering community. There is no rank or status here. Call no man father . . . All ye are brethren.

"Get This Message Going"

Get This Message Going

Toward the close of the 1989 Annual Council, work bogged down in questions of parliamentary procedure. The issue under discussion concerned the role of women in ministry: Should associates in pastoral care who have been ordained as local elders be given the same ministerial privileges as their male counterparts? It was now about 9:30 p.m. on October 9, with time running out and much of the agenda untouched. Then Charles Bradford came to the microphone. Speaking without notes he galvanized the Council to action.

Well, Brother Chairman, I just wanted to make an appeal.

The North American Division officers and union presidents set up a special committee after the 1985 General Conference session to address this question that you read from the minutes—the matter of the authority or the functions of ministry that would be granted to commissioned ministers, those who were called "associates in pastoral care." That small committee—that committee that met—brought in a recommendation. We thought it was in harmony with what the General Conference session directed to us, and it essentially said that the associates in pastoral care would be given authority to perform the same functions as licensed ministers.

We did that in good faith, but it was felt by some that it might be precipitous to bring it in to the 1985 Annual Council session and so we turned away from it. One union having seen it in the materials that you distribute, in the book, thought it was passed, went back home, and almost directed its conferences to act accordingly. I was embarrassed when they called me. I had to tell them that we pulled it off.

Some of you were there in 1985 when we pulled it back and you were disappointed. Some said to me, "You have not carried out the directive of the General Conference. You had it in the materials for distribution, you withdrew it." I really could not give any reasons other than I was counseled to do it. We accepted the counsel, and we did not press the matter.

It was thought that going this route would be better. It would give the world church an opportunity to hear, to consider, to empathize with, to better understand, and that has been done. The Commission met March of the year before and met again this summer. It has been on the minds, and I say on the lips of many for a number of years—almost, Brother Chairman, a decade. Now, Bill Bothe, you could say it as the man says on his epitaph, "Where you are, I once was. And where I am, you will be." You can say that, Bill. All of us are traveling toward a certain point. Meantime, we are still discussing, we are still discussing.

It is a terrible burden to try to lead a division in soul winning when you are constantly discussing these all-consuming issues. Now this division—any time you say "Amen" you give me courage. (Detamore called it artificial inspiration. Detamore came to one of the congregations

"GET THIS MESSAGE GOING"

where E. E. Cleveland was preaching and said, "If I got the artificial respiration like that, I could preach like you do"). But here we are in 1989 facing the last decade in the twentieth century—we are on the eve of the third millennium. That is where we are.

We have discussed this matter and discussed it, and people have taken sides and some have said, "I am not going to lose. I will use every ruse that I can, every political, every parliamentary motion and maneuver, I will use it so I will not lose. I will have my way." I would hope that in the church of the living God we could come to the place where it would not be a win/lose situation.

Now your humble servant after a little word that the brethren gave me opportunity to say on Thursday said, "Not another word," because I knew it would not sway anybody one way or the other. I do not want to inflame anybody, and I had to tug at myself to speak tonight because I know it will be misunderstood. Some will think I am grandstanding or playing to the galleries, but let me speak on.

This North American Division is the tax base of the world church. If the superstructure outgrows its tax base, we have a tottering institution. I speak plainly, I speak boldly, I say that if we do not get on with the mission here in North America and start winning people to this message as we should be, the church is going to suffer all around the world.

There is nothing wrong with this North American Division that a hundred thousand fully instructed, born again, new believers could not solve. The tithe dollar is the transaction that has the greatest impact upon this world church. When I baptize—and it is going to be my privilege and a happy circumstance, I hope, in a few days to do that more and more—when I baptize that dear little sister down in whatever little city it is, maybe she is on welfare, but when she comes to church on Sabbath morning, she makes

THE WIT AND WISDOM OF BRADFORD

out her little tithe envelope and she puts in $10 tithe and $2 winds up in Silver Spring, Maryland. That's *impact*. Giant Food only gets a dollar and a half out of a hundred or more. That's right.

This church has the greatest system in the world, but do you know what we are doing? We are destroying it. That is what we are doing. We are destroying it. In the North American Division, we have been distracted. Our attention has been taken away from the vital things.

There are those who stand up and say, "I am orthodox." Show me the souls that have been baptized by your pronounced orthodoxy. There is such a thing as dead orthodoxy. The rabbis could quote the Pentateuch, but they were not, my friends, alive with a vital religion that satisfies the longings of men's hearts.

We are going to make ourselves such an ingrown group—navel gazing, looking at our own problems, introspection—until we will wind up simply keepers of the museum. We will have artifacts of the past, we will have monographs on the administration of Wilson, Pierson, and Figuhr. That is all that will be left. We will not have a vibrant, growing church.

It is a serious word that I speak. Jesus is coming soon. There are some people out there who are counting on you to lead them in ministry. There are some people who would be ashamed that we are spending God's holy money and holy time in several days in Annual Council and yet we have not come to the things that brought us here. We have held up the agenda. You are going to make it almost impossible even for us to have a North American year end meeting this year.

Now my brothers and my sisters, the time has come. We must put aside all our preferences. I said to the division brethren—Elder Wilson, you allowed me to say it at Cohutta—I said to them, "Brethren, will this provision made for commissioned ministers damage your field? Will it bring

"GET THIS MESSAGE GOING"

you to ruin? If it will, we will turn aside."

They said, "No, it won't."

I said, "Well, then, it will not damage your fields, allow the church to roll on. Let the church move on."

If we have made a horrible mistake, there is such a thing as the Spirit's ministry, and He will bring us back because, as Ellen White says, we are captives of hope. He has us in His hands. We are the remnant people of God.

Oh, I want us to march on. I want to hear the words of God ringing throughout the North American Division, ringing throughout the world. I want to see the ministers on fire and the laymen going from door to door and this continent stirred from stem to stern so that the brethren in other denominations will say, "You Adventists have filled this whole continent with your doctrine." That is what I want to see happen.

But it will never happen as long as we are standing on this line and you are on that line. I think it is time to get on God's line. Will you please, brethren, have mercy upon us? For mercy is needed. You brethren need to pray for the North American Division. Pray for us.

I am begging your pardon for taking your time, but this is the way that I feel. I can but say what is on my heart. I would think that after 43 years, you would allow me for one night to say what is on my heart, to make a strong appeal to you, a fervent appeal.

Here we were on the sports thing nearly all day. Children dying with AIDS, children into drugs, teenage pregnancy, and we are arguing about a basketball game. I want to tell you if the religion in our churches were vibrant enough, a hint to the wise is sufficient. All you have to do is say, "Brethren and sisters, love not the world, neither the things that are in the world. If any man love the world, the love of the Father is not in him."

Those who are in tune with Heaven will say, "Look, I don't love the world anymore. I will turn away from these things." You can make a thousand pronouncements that will not change one heart.

So let's get on God's side, here. Get this message going. Don't you want to see the message go, Bill? I mean, we can do it. We can preach this message. We have the greatest message in the world. I want us to join together. I would be so happy if I can say then, "Let now thy servant depart in peace."

Anecdotes

Feeling Like It

Harry Emerson Fosdick said his dad used to tell him when he left in the morning, "Harry, mow the lawn if you feel like it." Then as he got to the curb he would turn around and say, "But be sure that you feel like it!"

G. P. C.

The early days after slavery—Reconstruction—is a rich, historical mine. So many people wanted to go back to school, so many were feeling the urge to travel. John Hope Franklin is the best scholar on that period. He was once chairman of the Department of History at the University of Chicago. He was also at Howard University in the history department and at other big universities.

During Reconstruction, Booker T. Washington says that many Black men felt the call to preach the gospel. In fact, the call would come to them sometimes in charismatic ways. They would fall prostrate in church. That is something that happened in colonial America and later post-revolutionary and frontier America. In those tremendous revivals people would be "slain of the Lord." Under the movement of the Spirit, they would fall out and then they would ask to preach a trial sermon. The churches always gave them opportunity to do so. This would determine if the "call" was genuine or not.

On one such occasion, the brother was evidently not called to preach. He was such a poor speaker. A dear old lady said to him after the service, "Son, how do you know you are called to preach?"

"Well," he said, "I saw a sign in the sky that said G.P.C."

"Well, what does that mean?" the old saint asked.

"Go preach Christ!"

"No, it doesn't mean that—it means "Go Plant Corn!"

If you are in the deep South, you can say "Go Plow Cotton." Those kinds of experiences frightened Booker T. Washington. He didn't want to preach. He was afraid everytime he went to church that he would fall out and be called to preach.

Watching That Little Bird

We had a problem in our conference. We were trying to counsel a young man—a preacher—and evidently it wasn't going home. Sometimes you can talk and people don't hear.

F. L. Peterson told a story, trying to help the fellow rather than counsel him, but he wasn't listening. Elder Peterson said, "Grandmother was talking to her grandson [it's always grandmother taking care of the grandson], but the little fellow wasn't paying any attention to her counsel. He let her know it by saying, 'Grandmommie, you know you've been talking a long time, but all the while I've been watching that little bird and he hasn't moved yet.' "

I don't know whether it helped the preacher or not. Peterson could tell those things when appropriate and anybody with any sense would know that what he was saying is, "You haven't heard a thing we've said, you've been watching that little bird."

Now I Understand

This one has been told in many settings, but for Adventist preachers it's the worker's report. You have to fill it in to get the check.

This man won't fill in his report. They threaten him, do everything they can, but still he won't fill it in. Finally they take him to the president and he says, "You fill in that blank or you are discharged."

"Oh," the man says, "no one ever explained it to me like that before. Now I understand."

This Head?

Dad was quite a fighter for his own rights. During the days in New Rochelle, New York, our members worked in very fine homes. Sometimes folks would say, "We only work for the best people." They called the people that worked in homes "domestics." As my father went around to see them, the people they worked for got to know him also.

One time this rich man said, "Well, preacher, I want to give you some hats." As my dad was going back to his car with the hats, a policeman stopped him. He called him some kind of too familiar name, wanted to know who he was, and generally hassled him. My dad made that policeman arrest him. The policeman said, "I don't want to bother you."

"No, you take me down to the station now."

So they took him down to White Plains in New Rochelle. The sergeant heard everything and he told the policeman, "Don't you bother that preacher anymore." The policeman got a tongue lashing.

Dad was good for that kind of debate, showing him not to play with him—he wasn't a child.

My sister married very young at Harlem Academy and her

husband was deported before their second child was born. He was taken up on the street, put on the boat, and sent back to Barbados, just like that. So my sister was left alone and she was just a young kid. She came to stay with us in New Rochelle. She tried to work and take care of the children.

She had a bill she owed for milk. In those days the milkman and the breadman would come by the house.

This man came and tried to get smart with my dad about his daughter's bill. He said something about knocking him in the head.

You didn't tell my dad that. Dad put his head right on him, right in his face, and said, "This head?" He was daring him to hit him. He said, "Not this head, no siree!"

The man backed away and got out of there. He was too frightened. I think my father finally said, "You see this foot?"

The Johnstown Flood

The Johnstown Flood was the greatest natural disaster of American history. Walls of water, tons and tons, thousands upon thousands of gallons rushed down and swept everything away. Few people survived.

This brother survived and forever after he told the story. It became *his* story. I suppose he embellished it. After having told it at conventions and wherever you must tell stories, he gets to heaven and tells St. Peter, "Please, I want to tell the story of the Johnstown Flood."

The crowd is excited. Peter says, "You may, but remember, Noah is in the audience."

Preaching Love for Five More Minutes

In the hills of Appalachia they used to build brush arbors for their revivals. They put up poles and took the leaves just like the children of Israel and made a shelter. The people would sit there in the shade and the old circuit-riding preacher would preach to them.

ANECDOTES

The people in those areas are pretty tough. On one occasion the parson was preaching too long so they began telling him to stop. But he kept on preaching. They threw up a little something at him—an orange, a tomato, whatever. But the old preacher wiped it away patiently and kept on preaching and preaching.

Finally he closed his Bible and said, "Brothers and sisters, I'm going to preach on brotherly love for about 5 more minutes, and if this mess don't stop coming up here there's going to be one of the biggest dog fights you ever saw in your life. The audience quieted down."

Morehouse and Your House

Martin Luther King Junior's father was a great preacher also. He was a graduate of the famous Morehouse College and didn't mind telling people about "When I was at Morehouse." One day a pastor friend of his came to his church to speak for a revival—another Morehouse graduate. So all week it was, "When we were at Morehouse, when we were at Morehouse," and so on.

During the devotional, they asked the deacon to give the prayer. He was the greatest praying deacon of his day, and he began by saying—speaking very slow, deliberately, like Churchill—"Oh Lord, I've never been to Morehouse, but I'm trying to go to Your house."

That affected King in a powerful way. It was a sermon for him. The deacon was serious about it. He was telling the pastor in his own way and in behalf of the church that we've had enough of this.

The Right Train

Elder H. D. Singleton was a great administrator and a chooser of men. He knew how to select talent and ability, and he chose several of the outstanding leaders of that day.

But he was also super cautious. He didn't rush into

anything. When he went to New York where there were subway trains, they didn't know him too well. He had been in the South all the time. He followed H. L. Bland who had a tremendous personality, with charisma and charm—a man people gravitated toward.

Singleton would interrogate the workers up and down and then he would go around and ask people about them. He would get all kinds of opinions—second, third, fourth opinions. And then finally he would hire the person or call them. So this got to be a legend.

One of the young preachers said, "You know, Sing may miss a lot of trains, but he never gets on the wrong one."

That's pretty good advice for an administrator today. Administrators need to check out the people that they hire. In North America today we have too much picking up people on the word of some person who really doesn't know, or on personal feelings, or on assessment without a basis of fact. That has hurt our work.

Singleton might make you a little upset, but he wouldn't choose the wrong person. If he chose you, you could know he had searched it out very carefully.

He Can't Do That Every Sabbath

My dad was quite a fellow. He was pastor at the Ephesus Church in Washington, D. C.

There was a tremendous orator among us by the name of J. G. Dasent. He used to put his thumbs in his pockets when he preached. He was of British background from the West Indies and had a stentorian bass voice. He wrote out his sermons and memorized a lot of the passages and he was careful in his delivery—he did everything properly. He had some moments of absolute brilliance. He talked once about the United Nations becoming the "united notions." He gave those prophetic kinds of sermons that we used to preach in those days.

Well, my dad used to have his friends come and

preach. Ephesus was one of the prominent churches: it was the church of what E. Franklin Fraizer, the great sociologist at Howard University, called the Black bourgeois. Everyone wanted to pastor that church. Dr. Dykes attended there, so did the Montgomery family, and a lot of people who were prominent in government.

So dear Brother Dasent came to preach for Pappa that day, and he gave a spellbinding oration. One of his better ones. People were elated and my dad saw them reacting. As my friend Gardner Taylor says, "A chorus of hallelujahs went up."

It is alleged that my dad got up and said, "Don't get excited, folks, he can't do that every Sabbath!"

After I was a full grown man and dad was retired, I asked him if he really said that. He wouldn't say yes or no. But knowing my dad he may have, because quite often he would say what came to his mind.

J. G. Dasent

People would say to J. G. Dasent at the door, "Elder Dasent, you preached such a good sermon today."

Sometimes he would reply, "I, J. Gershon Dasent, know I preached a good sermon."

He was a great character—an evangelist, a pastor, a builder. He came to Oakwood College once and gave the commencement address. He had on his morning trousers and cutaway coat. He got up, looked around, and said, "When I received the invitation to come and give this commencement address, I asked myself why I should disturb my tranquility by coming down to Alabama." He spoke with just a little disdain, but it was acceptable because he was who he was and, as we say, he could get away with it.

He counseled me when I was going to a certain field as an evangelist. I was just a youngster and it was a new field to me altogether. I began telling him my plan and schedule for the cities I was going to evangelize. I was going to have a meeting here and a meeting there and another meeting in still another city. I had a goal to baptize so many here and baptize so many there, and baptize so many in someplace else.

He looked at me and said, "You had better start with the first one and baptize those there before you count your converts in the next place."

He observed a strange thing about the mentality of Adventists. He said, "When the pastor first comes, he is so wonderful—he's a 'godsent man.' After he's been there a little while he is 'pretty good.' Then after another period of time, 'Oh, he'll do.' The final question is, 'When is he going?' "

What Dasent was telling me was "Our people are geared to constant pastoral change." We have to live with that fact.

The Quartet

When J. L. Moran was president of Oakwood College, he organized singing groups and quartets to raise money. They went all over the country gathering funds for building programs and just to keep the college going.

When World War II was over and gas was no longer rationed, Elder Calvin E. Moseley formed a quartet. He wanted me to join it. I had just gotten a nice suit my dad had bought me. Moseley had auditions, but I wasn't able to make it. He tried to be nice to me and he said, "Well, son, with your nice black suit you look like you can sing, you stand like you can sing, you act like you can sing, but you just can't sing!"

Years later Dr. John Richard Ford commissioned a painting—it's a mural actually—for the wall in Blake Center. It begins with the *Morning Star* boat and has various scenes. Then it gets to the late 40s and shows the quartet. But I'm missing. So I tell my grandchildren, "There is where your granddaddy would be, but for a voice."

Humility

A budding young theologue ascends the spiral swallow's nest pulpit, and as he passes by the old sexton he hardly notices him because he is so filled with his own importance. But evidently his sermon gets no response—it goes over like a dud. He comes down dejected.

Then the sexton has his opportunity to comment. He says, "If you had of went up like you came down, then you could have come down like you went up."

The Whole Load

H. M. S. Richards told this one—it's from the old West.

The preacher went to church on Sabbath (or Sunday, as the case may be) and found only one person there—an old rancher. But he preached and preached and preached and preached and kept on preaching. Finally he asked the old rancher how he did and the rancher said, "You did right well, but I'll tell you, if only one cow came for the feeding, I wouldn't give him the whole load!"

That Little Piece

Mother is feeding Johnny and Jimmy. There is a piece of pie and each, of course, thinks that mother treats the other one better. So Jimmy looks at this piece of pie and he says, "Oh, you gave Johnny that big piece of pie."

She says, "No, that's yours."

Quick as a flash he says, "What, that little piece?"

What?

Halford Luccock told about the old saint in the desert of Arabia or North Africa. He withdrew from the community and just fasted and prayed to be purified. And he did well. He resisted all the sins of the flesh, all the terrible sins that they list.

But finally the devil came to him with the most subtle temptation of all. "Did you hear? They just made your brother the bishop of Alexandria."

He said, "What? How could they overlook a saint like me?"

He was concerned that his brother would be chosen before him. So pride was still there even after all his fasting and his praying.

Assorted Sayings

They gave him an unlimited budget and he exceeded it!

It's very hard to prophesy and especially about the future.

Sincerity is the main thing; when you can fake that you've got it made.

Speaking from the General Conference standpoint. . . .

You may have been a headache, but you've never been a bore.

As the hypochondriac's headstone read: "Now you will believe me."

Telling you that is like preaching to Noah about the flood.

Some preachers use the same text and change their sermon; others use the same sermon but change the text.

Don't confuse me with the facts.

I may be standing on my feet, but I'm sitting down in my mind.

You're not on my little mind, let alone, my big mind.

It's not everything—it's the only thing.

Don't get mad—get smart.

Administration is the art of inflicting pain.

Politics is the art of the possible.

I'm from Washington and I'm here to help you.

You can't teach height.

Nevertheless, to the contrary, notwithstanding. . . .

That's the kind of stuff up with which I have to put.

The Sabbath in Africa

The Sabbath in Africa

The Sabbath is embedded in the culture of Africa. Ellen White gives us a clue in *The Great Controversy,* pages 577, 578. She tells us there that the history of the churches of Ethiopia and Abyssinia is especially significant. She tells how amid the gloom of the Dark Ages the Christians in Central Africa maintained their faith in the Sabbath. She describes how Rome learned of what they were doing and eventually beguiled them into acknowledging the Pope as an equal of Christ. Even though the Christians for some time came under the authority of Rome, when they got the chance they eventually threw off that yoke and returned to the Sabbath—though not in a pure form.

Elder Bekele Heye has written a master's thesis on this topic. The hordes of Islam were sweeping down into Africa. They cleaned out North Africa, which had the largest Christian centers. Augustine, Bishop of Hippo, was in North Africa; so were Jerome and other great fathers of the church. Now the Moslems are coming down across Africa. They reach as far as Ethiopia, the last bastion of Christianity. There is no Christianity in the sub-Sahara.

THE WIT AND WISDOM OF BRADFORD

The emperor is besieged and doesn't know what to do. So he sends to Rome and asks for their help. The Pope sends in the Jesuits and Portuguese soldiers, and they get the emperor to agree to yield to the institution of Sunday. According to Bekele, a big fight breaks out in the hustings, but in the palace the nobility and the priests go along with the change. There is a struggle—not a brief one, but one that lasts for almost 100 years.

Finally a young king comes to the throne and says, "I'm going to restore the ancient faith." He expels the Jesuits and the people go back to the Sabbath—not the pure Sabbath, but to the observance of both Sabbath and Sunday.

In West African culture the old men are dying out who when questioned can take you back and say, "Yes, they observed, they held the seventh day in reverence." In West Africa, this custom has to be from primeval times—it is not of Hebrew extraction, as it is in Ethiopia.

We have to do more work in this. That's why I'm thinking about a project. Ellen White in *Fundamentals of Christian Education,* pages 374 and 375, challenges us to exercise our faculties. She says that when human agents do this, applying their knowledge to deep thinking, they will become the greatest witnesses for God and the truth, and even judges and kings will be brought to a knowledge of our great truths.

Gottfried Oosterwal agrees with me. He says his latest visit to Africa encouraged him to look further into this. If a people with a culture that is perhaps the oldest, going back to prehistoric times, not having interaction with other nations, if these people have knowledge of a day which is kwami's—the name they have for the highest god in their pantheon—that is something significant.

I want to see a research center at Oakwood College for this. I want to encourage our young scholars to get into it.

I can preach this. I have preached this for many years as I talk about the change of the Sabbath. Black people say,

THE SABBATH IN AFRICA

"But this Saturday is White folks' day."

I say, "Oh no, you'd better go back to your real roots. Your fathers who came from Africa had the knowledge of all this." Then I invite them to return to the faith of their fathers.

J. N. Andrews did his best in his *History of the Sabbath,* but look at the tools we have today. We could bring them together and present material to challenge the greatest minds. Ellen White is telling us to do research. The kids have the minds and the tools to do it. We need to challenge them. We need anthropologists of the first order to go in and handle the material, analyze it, put it in order so it is impeccable. Then probably we should have a conference and invite all sorts of people—not just Adventists—to it.

Ethel

Ethel

Ethel is the great joy of my life. She's a practical woman. She is a level-headed person. She's unflappable.

If she were to say "amen" out loud in church, I would be afraid. I've never heard her say one amen in church. She's not responsive in that way. She comes from a family that is very low key. They are not gushing, not all running over everyone, they are very reserved and careful. Her mother was that way, her father was that way, her sister too. But they are deeply committed to those they believe in and love.

And they are never given over to flattery. Never! If I may say so, I have often wanted them to come and say, "That was a great sermon you preached today. You did this or that or the other." Ethel does that a little more now than before, but often I have to call for it or beg for it. I don't know if she didn't want to spoil me or she just didn't feel that way, but she has never given over to pouring it on. That's just the way it is. But in the lurch, she is absolutely as constant as the North Star.

I suppose that is what I need. None of us knew

ETHEL

anything about marriage when we got married. We didn't know how to seek out a mate. We read *Messages to Young People* or whatever they had, and we went to a ministerial seminar when they put on a program on what to look for in a mate, the minister's wife and all that.

That was the biggest night, the Friday night when they told us they were going to discuss the minister's wife. Everybody would show up—ministerial students, girls who wanted to marry preachers, everybody was there. I don't know that any of those suggestions ever helped us. I guess some of us were just lucky.

I was fortunate enough to have a wife who could play the piano. She never was a public person. This is why I say, let a woman be what she is. We must not try to cut every minister's wife out of the same bolt of cloth. They must be genuine, they must love their husbands and support their spouses and give them counsel.

Ethel never attended a single board meeting. She has never been a great Bible instructor, in and out of homes and all that. But she has had the ability to keep the home on an even keel. That's what it's all about. Not some typical minister's wife that you read about, not some composite put together that does this, does that, and so forth. It's never been like that at all.

So in our earlier days in the churches where there was no musician, she could play. Sometimes when we had some reluctant, even recalcitrant pianists, that seemed to spur them on to greater effort and even cooperation!

I never bothered her about writing out my sermons. I scribbled them down on paper. Sometimes she has taken shorthand and notes for me.

But she's a great girl. I have a little joke I play on her sometimes. I say, "You give these children everything." So I tell a story—at the wedding I am overlooked. I just happen to be part of the group. Everybody is looking at the bride and the women. When the baby is born—I'm on the sidelines again. Everyone comes up to the mother and says, "Oh, you have a baby!" When the daughter gets married, mother is still up front. Now here come the grandchildren. I guess I'll never have my day.

But she laughs with me and says, "I know that you don't mind too much what I do for them."

I can't say enough about Ethel. Her ministry was not spectacular. She wanted it that way, I suppose. She is much more into the workings of the church now. She has keen perception. She can tell you what the brethren are doing, and she cannot understand the charade, as she calls it, the games that the brethren are playing. She wants them to come down nice and neat, black and white, right and wrong. Why don't you do this or that? Why do you string along, and talk and talk and talk and so forth? She has things pretty well categorized, and knows what is happening in the church.

Her mother had that gift too. There was a certain minister who had a psychological problem. Long before anyone knew about it, her mother said, "Elder so and so has a little problem, doesn't he?"

Ethel is excellent at reading people. I've given up on trying to put things over her, because she knows it anyway!

"You Will Be Missed, Charlie Lee"

"You Will Be Missed, Charlie Lee"

I'm glad to hear some calling him "Charlie Lee," because that's what I've known him as for about 50 years.

And his passing, his death, has sent shock waves throughout the Adventist community, worldwide. But the epicenter of that fearful shock is right here—in this family. What a marvelous family! Look what you did, Pop and Mom—a marvelous family!

It is felt more keenly in the ranks also of his fellow workers. Charles used to sing,

"Preachers and teachers would make their appeal
Fighting like soldiers on life's battlefield.
When to their pleading, my poor heart would yield.
All I could say, there's something within."

And so they have stood with him, shoulder to shoulder, all over the globe—planet earth, as he liked to say—preaching, teaching, calling. Modeling the gospel. Heralding the soon return of the coming King.

And we are moved. All of us are affected profoundly. We are numbed. We are groping for words, for understanding. We want to derive some meaning from this. We're

THE WIT AND WISDOM OF BRADFORD

thinking, *What is it going to be without Charlie Lee?* What will it be like in the family circle, in the church at large?

Jonathan's words to David are so appropriate. Jonathan is sending out his buddy to be hunted like a bird of prey by his father, insanely jealous and envious of the budding rising star, of whom the people said, "Saul has slain his thousands but David his ten thousands." David was innocent but he had to flee, spend the better part of many years in his long life in exile, forced to feign madness at one time in the Philistine camp.

It's hard to explain it. So many of God's servants have suffered for no apparent reason to us. Some are living and doing well who, if we had our way, we would exchange for this brother here today. Some are still enemies of the gospel, still bringing division in Christ's body. Yet a servant like this, who knew nothing but love, is laid to rest.

Let us not trivialize this matter. Let us not as preachers offer this family some half-baked theology, some reason which makes God complicit. The enemy has moved people to write in insurance policies, "An act of God." As C. S. Lewis says, "God is in the dock." He's on trial. He's been charged with insensitivity, with ignoring the plight of children and helpless people.

It was not David's fault, but Jonathan sent him out and he said, "Tomorrow is the festival of the new moon. We'll all be around Dad's table." "But," he said, "you will be missed, because your seat will be empty" (2 Kings 20:18).

Committees, boards, staff meetings, George Knowles, workers' meetings, conventions, devotions at the General Conference office, seminars and workshops, pulpits all around the world—there will be an empty chair. At the table, Gladyce, the hearth. It is not easy. I bring you no pablum here this afternoon, no little placebo to take down with a little milk and water. It is real.

There is one thing that God taught our people in times past, in hard days, and that was: Never deny the reality of

"YOU WILL BE MISSED, CHARLIE LEE"

death. Do not accommodate it. Do not try to wish it away by saying, "It is just now the slumber room that we visit. The deceased expired." Death has become the modern obscenity. And so people in these times sedate themselves so heavily and deny, deny, deny. And the psychiatrist says, "I'll have to see them later."

But in the days of our parents, when they had to work in the fields, they only had one day to bury their dead. They had the wake that night. And the master looking on said, "Those people are acting crazy. They're crying. They're showing emotion." And then the old preacher would stand and say, "He's dead. She's dead. Dead." And after their pent-up emotions were given expression, the next day they were back in the fields. They needed no psychiatrist.

You'll be missed, Charlie Lee. Your seat will be empty, especially at the coming General Conference session. The president of the General Conference has already expressed his sense of loss.

Now this preacher has been asked by the family and by Charles' prearrangement to speak some words of comfort. But frankly, the preacher needs words of comfort himself. The preacher sought out to find acceptable words. He has a fairly adequate library. But all the words I could get from Barth, Brunner, Bultman, and even Kubla-Ross, and the rest seemed like ashes on the altar. The preacher confesses that there is nothing within himself that can bring adequate comfort to you.

Charlie Lee used to sing this one, too—"In times like these." We need more than pious platitudes, shallow prefabricated glib answers to hard questions. This is a tough one. So we need powerful words. Supernatural words. Transcending words. Words out of eternity into time. Words that don't die with the latest score at the ballgame.

"The words that I speak unto you," He said, "they are spirit. They are life." So He said to this Charles, "I have

THE WIT AND WISDOM OF BRADFORD

some words for you to share with them." Where could I go but to the Lord?

And so here it is, the Epistle to the Hebrews the sixth chapter, verse 17. Words! "Because God wanted to make the unchanging nature of His purpose very clear to the heirs of what was promised, He confirmed it with an oath." He swore. God swore, took an oath. "He did this so that by two unchangeable things, in the which it is impossible for God to lie, we who have fled to take hold of the hope offered to us may be greatly encouraged."

We have this hope. I didn't know the choir was going to sing this today. We have this hope as an anchor for the soul. Firm and secure. It enters the inner sanctuary, behind the curtain. The King James says, "within the veil."

Who cares what veil it is? Seventh-day Adventist scholars have been fighting for years—theological sword battles—over whether it was the first veil or the second veil. No matter what veil it is, the point of the whole question is that the veil has been rent in twain. And He's gone on in. We can follow Him.

Powerful words! He entered on our behalf. He has become a high priest forever—forever! He has an unchangeable priesthood in the order of Melchezidek, with rank and status and ambassadorial credentials. He is God's plenipotentiary. He can go anywhere, He can do anything—all power not some power but all power, is in His hands. Soul anchor is what I call it. Soul anchor.

I read some time ago about a traveler in Switzerland who asked a little Swiss child, "Do you know where Kondestag is?"

The little child answered, "I do not know where Kondestag is, but there is the road."

You see, we're facing the ultimate here—issues of life and death and eternity and immortality. We're talking also about what theologians call theodicy—the justice of God, the vindication of God. It comes as a surprise to many, but

"YOU WILL BE MISSED, CHARLIE LEE"

God needs vindicating because He's been falsely charged. Intelligent answers to these ultimate questions are beyond our ken. I can't give you all the answers. That's what I want to tell you frankly—I can't give you all the answers. It has not been revealed unto me why Charles had to die, why I'm still living. I can't give you all the answers to these questions that haunt us, that put themselves before us. I can't do it.

But I came here this afternoon to tell you that there is the Way. There is the Truth. There is the Life. God's personal answer to life's dilemma and unanswered questions. No man comes to the father but by Him. He's gone before us. He's blazed the trail. In His own person He's the ultimate answer. The whole nature of God, you see, is involved in His promises. He's a God who makes promises. The poet Frost talked about promises to keep. Well, God has made promises.

One dear old Adventist saint—it must have been Loughborough or one of them—said, "I've been counting the promises of God lo these 40 years. I have not yet exhausted the word of God but I have come up by now with 3,000 of them. And of all the words the Lord has spoken, not one has fallen to the ground."

His nature, God's nature, is involved in His promises. And Jesus is the supreme pledge of God. By sending Him forth He vouchsafes to us that His promises cannot fail. He says, "I'm not going to explain everything to you. You couldn't understand it if I told you. But I will set forth someone who comes out of My bosom. Someone who is equal to Me. And He, in His own ministry, will declare unto you in unfailing ways that my promises cannot fail."

I was thinking just last night. Jesus descended into the grave where in a few moments we will place our brother's body. Think of it. He has already been there and blazed the trail, and opened the tomb. And He cannot lie. It is impossible, He said, for Him to lie. He promised and He swore—an oath—that He would keep that promise.

THE WIT AND WISDOM OF BRADFORD

Just yesterday doing a few errands getting ready for this occasion I turned on my car radio and there came a news item. A father decided to give his daughter a check for $25,000. He wrote the check for $25,000 (she's a grown daughter on her own, working, had her own home) and she decided to invest it. She went to her broker and bought some CD's and gave him the check for $25,000. He deposited it in his bank and then just before it cleared the father's bank, the old man passed away. And the bank reneged. The bank refused to make the check good. The newscaster went on to say that the case first reached the lower courts of Ohio. When it finally got to the State Supreme Court, the Court ruled for the bank—some foolish reasoning that I can't understand. They ruled for the bank against the woman!

Well, the news reporter tied it off like this: "When you accept a check, don't only look to see what the balance is in the bank, but examine the health of the person who wrote the check."

Ah, but I'm here to tell you today that the One who has written my check of salvation cannot lie and He cannot die. "I'm alive," He says, "forevermore. Death and hell cannot break my covenant." Adventist evangelists used to quote the passage in the Psalm where Yahweh says through David, "My covenant I will not break, nor alter the thing that has gone out of My lips."

You can count on it. The bank of heaven will never renege on a check that is written and signed by Jesus Christ. And so God says, "If I should break my pledged word, I should cease to be God. My very nature would dissolve." If God ever lied, then you could preach that God is dead.

Then He said, "You fled for refuge here." This is Sanctuary language. I still preach the Sanctuary, because I need the Sanctuary. Talk about Noriega needing a sanctuary, I need a sanctuary. Ah, what more can He say than to you He has said, who unto the Saviour for refuge hath fled.

"YOU WILL BE MISSED, CHARLIE LEE"

He has prepared a city of refuge for me. He has prepared a sanctuary for me. And when I'm harried and harrowed by the enemy, when I'm wounded and driven like a bird of prey, He opens the door and says, "Come on inside, into my sanctuary, and take hold of the horns of the altar."

And there are two cables. One that assends and another that descends. And will the cable break? Oh, no. And the anchor will always hold. It will not slip. It will not drag. The anchor holds.

Twin cables. One would have been enough, but He wanted to assure us so He says, "I'll give you a second one." As one of our United States presidents used to say, "Let me make this perfectly clear." We must make this very clear.

One preacher put it this way. There's a little boat floating on the sea. A storm is churning the waters. There's a powerful whirlpool and the little boat is getting closer to the vortex. The oars are gone, the motor is gone—drowned out, and there they are helpless on this little craft. Along comes a Coast Guard cutter. It can't get close enough to anchor this little boat and so they pick the strongest swimmer on board. They wrap a line around him and tie it. He jumps into the angry waters, swims to the little outboard motor boat, secures the rope to the boat, swims back to the big cutter and ties the rope to the larger craft. In the incarnation and ascension—the Christ event—He came down with the rope and he goes up with the rope and nobody can touch that rope! It is secure.

He will come again. Seventh-day Adventists have been proclaiming this for lo these years and this message is just as relevant and even more so than it ever has been. That is why God raised us up. He saw a people before they knew themselves. He called one out of a city, two out of a country. He raised them up and He said to them, "You will be my witnesses that no matter how dark the night, no matter how widespread the iniquity, there will come a day when the lights will go on all over again."

THE WIT AND WISDOM OF BRADFORD

Our family once visited Carlsbad Caverns in New Mexico. We went deep down into the bowels of the earth. They led us into the Rock of Ages Cathedral where we sat in pitch darkness. The story is told of a little girl who sat with her brother there, just the two of them. He began crying, so she patted his hand and began to say, "Don't cry, brother, there's a man here that knows how to turn the lights on."

> "It will firmly hold in the straits of fear,
>   When the breakers tell that the reef is near;
>   Though the tempest rage and the wild winds blow,
>   Not an angry wave shall our bark o'erflow.
>   It will surely hold in the floods of death,
>   When the waters cold chill our latest breath;
>   On the rising tide it can never fail,
>   While our hopes abide within the veil.
>   When our eyes behold in the dawning light,
>   Shining gates of pearl, our harbor bright,
>   We shall anchor fast to the heavenly shore,
>   With the storms all past forevermore."

We only have a downpayment now. This is the earnest of our redemption. But the full reality is sure to come. God has pledged His Word. He will settle the issue.

Your children look for their promised Christmas toys. They want them, they anticipate them, they imagine themselves playing with them. But when they open the wrapper, when they see the real thing, it is far beyond their expectations.

The little street urchin stood gazing in the window of the big department store. It is Christmas Eve, and the store is about to close. His nose is almost pressed to the glass, close enough to frost the windowpane. Then a big man comes along. He's well dressed, with a cashmere coat on. And he says, "Little fellow, would you like to have that toy?"

"Yes, Mister, but you wouldn't kid me, would you?"

"YOU WILL BE MISSED, CHARLIE LEE"

"No, I'm not kidding you." He took him in, bought it, gave it to him, and as he went bounding down the street everyone could hear him saying, "Now you're mine, all mine. And there's no glass between."

And I shall see Him, face to face, and there will be no glass between. No sea to separate us. Nothing between my soul and my Saviour.

I say to you, that people all over this North American Division and around the world are moved by this event. It may be, brother preacher, that God is trying to tell us something. The things of earth will dim and lose their value. They only last for a while.

I'm here to tell you, the older you get the less your tastebuds will respond. You will become jaded and satiated. And you will become almost tired as it were of the same round. You will be as the wise man said, "afraid of that which is high." You'll get to the place where you stumble over an electric cord—can't step over it.

My poor daddy used to follow me around. He was an old retired preacher and wanted to go everywhere I went. Sometimes I wasn't as kind as I should have been. I was about my duties, about my Master's business. He would take so long getting in and out of the car. I said, "Papa, why is it that it takes you so long to get in and out?"

He said, "I can't explain it to you, Son, but keep on living."

Now I have said already that the shock waves have gone out and the lives of many, multiplied thousands, are touched, as the intelligence races from state to state and capital to capital, and conference office or union office, and institution to institution, because they all knew him. They all loved him. I can't understand how he could have an enemy in the world. There are some of us who can understand why we may have one or two. But not him. Not the man who never said No. Not the man who went when he was sick. Not the man who smiled when he felt bad. Not the man who encouraged you when he already had reason to be down—not that man.

A church member in California, who never knew Charles, heard about his death. She didn't think much about it at first, but she couldn't sleep. As she lay awake that night she put pen to paper. "I must write something," she said to herself. And write she did—for the family, for all of you. The title is "Silver Chords."

"Silver Chords"*
Silver chords—
O wondrous design;
Delicate vibrations
Intricately combine
To produce sounds for myriad of songs;
    Songs that speak to our hearts.
His silver chords
Were finely tuned and rare;
    The tessitura webbed within the
    Timbre of his voice,
    Pulsated smoothly through the air,
    Like one perfect strain.
The soul rejoiced;
    Light streaming in
Bade darkness depart,
    When golden tones touched
    Responsive hearts.
    In true bel canto form,
    Melodious themes were oft'times expressed,
    In songs of happiness—
    "In My Heart There Rings a Melody"
    In words of personal action—
    "So Send I You"
    Pleadingly—
    "If With All Your Heart Ye Truly Seek Me"
    Knowingly—

"YOU WILL BE MISSED, CHARLIE LEE"

"He Touched Me"
Grand refrains
Refreshed the soul again and again!
Yet, humility personified his spirit
Where ere he trod.
The generous sharing of his gift,
Raised our conscious levels,
Even to the Throne of God.
And hearing there innumerable voices
(erelong)
Angels will cease their praises;
The redeemed will sing their song;
When the note will be struck higher,
Than any earthly tone can achieve,
May his silver chords now loosed
Respond in endless cadence,
Throughout eternity!
And forever, and forever, and forever. World without end. That silver voice will never be hushed again. Higher and higher until angels fold their wings, for angels never knew the joy that our salvation brings.
Let's meet him, what do you say? Let's meet him.

---

* By Dr. Alice Smith, San Diego, California
(Dedicated to the family and friends of Elder Charles L. Brooks)

Sermons

"The Art of Being a Sinner"
(Good Man Last, Bad Man Saved) Luke 18:9-14

Jesus had to hang tough. The leaders of Jewish society were absolutely hostile and the plain people were misinformed and misled. His message was counter to rabbinic thought and teachings. So He takes up the form of a parable. He tells stories. He gets into their heads before they know it. As they lean forward, ears open to hear His spellbinding tale, their defenses fall. For a moment they relax and the Master teacher immediately thrusts in the sickle—the sharp sword of the Word. He knows his target audience. They trust themselves. They despise others. He will show that these despised others are nearer the kingdom than the teachers of the law.

In the parables we are standing right before the Saviour and He is reading us all the time. Our inmost thoughts are exposed. We see ourselves in the mirror of truth that He holds before us. No one can escape, even the Pharisee, the man who is high on the totem pole, the finest product of Jewish religion.

So He begins. There are these two men who go up to the temple to pray—the one a Pharisee, the other a tax collector. The Pharisee prays with himself. He stands. He looks toward heaven. Quite at home in the temple—a longtime worshiper—his prayer is really a soliloquy. He thanks God he's not like other people, tells God all the good things he's done, and as he sees the poor tax collector come in he says, *even* this publican.

The poor tax collector who for some reason (perhaps moved upon by the Holy Spirit) has decided to attend the services at the temple that day is crushed, He has an overwhelming sense of his unworthiness, He really has no business here, he thinks to himself. "I have nothing to commend me to God. O, God," he says, "be merciful to me a sinner."

Then the quick thrust. Jesus says, "This man goes down justified rather than the other. Christ's hearers say, "How can this be?" Even the disciples ask "Who then can be saved? If this highest example of Jewish religion cannot be saved, what about us? Who in the world can make it?" But then they remember. Jesus said, "Except your righteousness shall exceed the righteousness of the scribes and Pharisees, ye shall in no case enter into the kingdom of heaven" (Matthew 5:20).

Now let me illustrate. Even before I was a teenager my mother would from time to time send me to the store to buy a few items. She made good yeast bread. And she was rather hung up on brand names. When it came to yeast, the brand was Fleischmann's. There was Red Star, and there were other brands, but only Fleischmann's. Sometimes I would be playing with my friends and she'd call, "Charles, go to the store and bring me a cake of Fleischmann's yeast. Only Fleischmann's."

But you know how boys are. We forget, even when we get to be big boys. And once or twice I brought back Red Star. Then she would say, "Just turn around and march yourself back to the grocery store and bring me what I asked you." That was the only brand that mother would accept.

Well, there's only one brand of righteousness that God will accept. Jesus is in no way condemning the Pharisee for the good things he's done. These are all commendable—tithing, fasting, abstinence from evil things, moral rectitude. This parable is the perfect vehicle for communicating the greatest truth. God accepts only one brand of righteousness—the impeccable, sinless life of His own obedient Son.

Paul saw this clearly. "And be found in Him, not having mine own righteousness, which is of the law, but that which is through the faith of Christ, the righteousness which is of God by faith" (Philippians 3:9).

I said reverently, God is hung up on brand names. It is the garment woven by His son in the loom of heaven. There is not one human thread in it. It is not my brand or yours, but His that counts.

A famous evangelist bought a diamond on the boardwalk in Atlantic City. He thought he had a bargain. Took it to his jeweler friend to set it for his wife. It was to be the perfect gift, the perfect ring. The evangelist was feeling good about it—the wonderful deal he had made, and all that—when his jeweler friend, after examining the stone with his magnifying glass, looked up and said, "It's worthless. I can't mount it."

"But," said the evangelist, "it looks so beautiful."

"Yes, to the naked eye. But there's a fatal flaw in the middle of it—right down the center. If I try to cut it, it will break into smithereens."

A brand of righteousness is needed that will pass the X-ray inspection of God's holy and awesome law. No matter how perfect the human righteousness, it cannot bear the inspection of heaven's royal law that reads the thoughts, the intents of the heart, weighs the motives, tests the commitment, searches us through and through, and demands perfection.

A good friend of mine was a tailor for Hart, Schaffner, and Marx. He knew the business. He knew fabric, design, everything that was necessary to make a quality suit. Once in a while a second would come through. He'd call me and ask if I wanted to look at it, to try it on, to see how I liked it. But he would always tell me, "Please remember, though, this suit is a second. It is not perfect. It only looks that way. Should a tailor examine it he could tell at once that there are some threads here that are imperfect. Perhaps the weaving or the color is not just right. I remember one particularly attractive suit that I bought from him at a very reasonable price. People admired it, but they did not know what I knew. It was a second.

And so our righteousness that we produce is always a second. It will not pass muster in heaven's court. We must reach out for that righteousness which is out of and beyond ourselves. Theologians have called it an "alien righteousness." I don't like that word, but what they mean, I suppose, is that it is something that does not spring out of human effort.

Then Jesus used the word "justification" here. This man went down to his house justified rather than the other. Who said there was no teaching of justification by faith in Christ's sermons? I could have well named this sermon, "For Preachers and Other Sinners." For as Ellen White says, "It is only he who knows himself to be a sinner that Jesus can save" (*Christ's Object Lessons,* p. 158). Here is the art of being a sinner, of recognizing one's unworthiness, of saying with Isaiah when he saw the holy God high and lifted up, "I am unworthy. I am unclean. I dwell in the midst of a people of unclean lips." And no matter how much progress we make in the Christian journey, we are still to admit, "I am a sinner." Humility is in order.

"Nothing in my hand I bring, simply to the cross I cling." Does this mean that I give in to the devil's promptings? Does this mean that I sin so that grace may abound? Does this mean that I do not strive to overcome? Certainly not. It does mean, however, that I am in a perpetual state of repentance and always keenly aware of the weaknesses of the flesh.

The old Black spiritual puts it this way: "Watch, my brother, how you walk on the cross. Your foot might slip and your soul get lost." "Let him that thinketh he standeth take heed lest he fall." The greatest of all apostles exclaimed, "Jesus came into the world to save sinners, of whom I am chief."

In Alcoholics Anonymous, they all confess, "I am an alcoholic." Some of them can testify, "I am in recovery." They have not had a drink in many years. But they recognize that they are still an alcoholic. The difference is they are in recovery.

Yes, we are sinners. Yes, we are saved by grace. But we also are kept by His power. "Now unto Him who is able to keep you from falling, and to present you faultless before the presence of His glory with exceeding joy" (Jude 24).

Many years ago a young man at one of our colleges gave me this illustration. A diabetic will always be a diabetic, but his daily injection of insulin helps him to perform. So we need our daily infusion of Christ's righteousness. His blood is the only antidote for sin and His Spirit the only power that can keep us from sinning. "But if we walk in the light, as He is in the light, we have fellowship one with one another, and the blood of Jesus Christ His Son cleanseth us from all sin" (1 John 1:7).

Those who are familiar with the New Testament Greek say the verse could well be rendered, "The blood of Jesus continually washes us from our sins." It is always needed.

Dr. A. T. Pierson, founder of the Christian and Missionary Alliance Church, sometimes used a wordplay of "in" and "on." He pictures the three crosses on Golgotha. On one, a man dies cursing, swearing, rejecting his Lord. This man, Dr. Pierson said, dies with sin on him and in him.

On the other cross, let's say on the left, a man dies confessing his sins and professing faith in the Saviour. He dies with no sin on him but sin is in him. He dies in a mortal body and has by no means completed his course in sanctification.

But the man in the middle cross, our Saviour, dies with

sin on him but not in Him. How can I say that Jesus died with sin on Him? Was He not the sinless son of God? Yes, but He took our sins upon Him—indeed, the sins of the whole world. But there was no sin in Him. He was holy, harmless, undefiled, separate from sinners. He worked out this impeccable righteousness during His human experience. He pitched His tent next to our tents, lived with us, and in a body of flesh lived in perfect obedience to His Father's will.

The sin that was on Him was not His own. And when we see Him dying for our sins and when we come to understand that He was perfect, without flaw, never for once out of harmony with His Father's law, then we cry out for His righteousness. It alone will suffice. Mine is as filthy rags. "My hope is built on nothing less than Jesus' blood and righteousness."

"Quick, the best robe"

Luke 15:22, *Today's English Version*.
"But the Father called to His servants. 'Hurry!' he said. 'bring the best robe and put it on him. Put a ring on his finger and shoes on his feet. Then go and get the prize calf and kill it, and let us celebrate with a feast! For this son of mine was dead, but now he is alive; he was lost, but now he has been found.' And so the feasting began."

The dirty, smelly boy comes home. All the hired hands and family members wait to see how dad is going to react. They know how they would react. They would scold him, maybe make him stay outside the gate for some time. Put him on probation. Make sure that his repentance is genuine, this boy who has caused his father such pain. The only news the old man ever received was from someone who saw him perhaps in a nightclub or at the race track. But the report that cut dad to the quick was when someone said, "I saw him in a pig sty."

Now the boy is at the gate and everybody is waiting to see what will happen. What a surprise when dad jumps up

THE WIT AND WISDOM OF BRADFORD

from his chair. He has been looking out the window. He runs like a youngster to meet his boy, tears running down his face. He holds him tight. "Oh, my son! Oh, my son!" he says.

The boy makes his heartfelt but simple confession. "I have sinned. I am not worthy to be called your son. Just make me a hired servant.

"A hired servant? No!" the father says, turning now to the crowd looking on. They are shocked—even traumatized. "Quick, the best robe. Bring it, put it on him, and put the ring on his finger and shoes on his feet. My son was lost and is found. He was dead, he's alive. Now let's celebrate. Let the feasting begin."

Jesus may have enjoyed this story best of all because it illustrates His favorite theme—the paternal character, the abundant love of God, His relationship to His earthborn children. But what a radical concept it is in contrast to the Pharisees, the teachers of his day, who pictured God as austere, a stern parent, inflexible, autocratic, judgmental. Jesus felt wounded because His Father was misunderstood and He wanted to set the record straight.

Here is the key to reading and understanding the Scriptures, the character of God, His paternal nature. Ellen White says this is the gift God gave to the world. This is the gift He has given to us and we must share this with the world. After all, Adventists must correct the misapprehension of the nature and character of God that is current in the world.

"Bring the best robe," he says. "Not that old tattered one, but the very best one I have." This son is to be restored. He is to be reinstated into the family. He is to be treated as if he had never left. He is fully accepted. He is a part of the family. And he must be more than simply tolerated. He is to enjoy the favor of his father, the love and respect of the entire family.

"And get the ring and put it on his finger." It is as if the father is saying, "You have authority. All the rights and privileges of this family are yours. You may use them." It needs to be said over and over again. To as many as received Him, to them gave He the right (the authority, the prerogative) to be called the sons and daughters of God" (John 1:12).

And they may use His name: "When that day comes, you will not ask me for anything. I am telling you the truth: the Father will give you whatever you ask of Him in My name. Until now you have not asked for anything in My name; ask and you will receive, so that your happiness may be complete." He puts a blank check in our hands and says, "Use it. Fill it in. It is My name that is signed there. Ask whatever you will." Again, we must make this clear. Clear to all who come to God by Him. By placing the ring on his hand, the father is saying to his son, "You are empowered to do business in my name. My bank account, my resources, all that I have, is shared with you."

"And put shoes on his feet." Sons must not go barefoot. The servants, the members of the household, must know that he is a son. He is not a slave. He is partner with his father. He must carry on the family traditions. He must do his part to build the estate. He is now a manager, a trustee, a steward. He must not simply enjoy his status, his name, the privileges, and the prerequisites that come with it. As a member of the family he has responsibilities. The father will give him an assignment. He will go into the vineyard and work. He will be faithful in carrying out these duties given him.

All that the father confers upon him—the robe, the ring—is to prepare him for service. His feet are shod with the preparation of the gospel of peace. His feet are shod that he may go and spread the good news. "But when the Holy Spirit comes upon you, you will be filled with power, and you will be witnesses for me in Jerusalem, and all of Judea and Samaria, and to the ends of the earth" (Acts 1:8, TEV).

We are amazed that God can receive the sinner, give him status, share His name with him, and make him a witness—an ambassador—of the kingdom. We can scarcely believe it. The plan of salvation is not simply to save the sons and daughters of Adam from eternal death. It is more than some clever way to "get us off the hook" or, as they say in common parlance, to "beat the rap." There is more than that. "Higher than the highest human thought can reach!" Abundantly above all that we could ask or think.

It is really the father who is prodigal, giving lavishly, forgiving unconditionally, restoring absolutely. It is God who so loves that He gives heaven's greatest and best gift to the human family. It is the heavenly Father who provides for us a mediator and a Saviour, who washes us in His precious blood, robes us in His righteous garment, and presents us to heavenly society with the request that we be accepted on His behalf. "The divine intercessor presents the plea that all who have overcome through faith in His blood be forgiven their transgressions, that they be restored to their Eden home, and crowned as joint heirs with Himself to 'the first dominion' (Micah 4:8) . . . He asked for His people not only pardon and justification, full and complete, but a share in His glory and a seat upon His throne" (*The Great Controversy*, p. 484).

Think of it: A share in His glory. I have no shares in General Motors, Chrysler, or Ford, but I do have a share in His glory. And then the ultimate. I am but a pilgrim and stranger here without recognition in the power centers of this world. But He has reserved for me a seat upon His throne. No wonder when the missionary faithfully presented this kind of God to his audience—loving, kind, paternal in nature, benevolent, aggressive in His love—the old African woman turned to her family and village friends and said, "See, I told you there had to be a God like that."